LAND OFFICE

AND

PREROGATIVE COURT RECORDS

OF

COLONIAL MARYLAND

BY

ELISABETH HARTSOOK

GUST SKORDAS

Southern Historical Press, Inc.
Greenville, South Carolina

This volume was reproduced
from a personal copy located in
the Publishers private library

Please direct all correspondence and book orders to:
SOUTHERN HISTORICAL PRESS, Inc.
PO Box 1267
Greenville, SC   29602-1267

Originally printed: Maryland 1949
ISBN #978-1-63914-140-1
Printed in the United States of America

TABLE OF CONTENTS

THE HALL OF RECORDS

The Hall of Records of Maryland was built as a part of the ter-centenary celebration of the landing of the *Ark* and the *Dove*. It is located in Annapolis on the corner of College Avenue and St. John's Street. It is controlled and supervised by the Hall of Records Commission which was created by Chapter 18, Acts of 1935, and which is composed ex-officio of the Governor, the Comptroller of the Treasury, the Chief Judge of the Court of Appeals, the Presidents of the St. John's College, the Maryland Historical Society, the Board of the Peabody Institute, and the Johns Hopkins University. The present members of the Hall of Records Commission are Governor Herbert R. O'Conor, the Honorable J. Millard Tawes, Jr., Judge Ogle Marbury, Chairman, Mr. Stringfellow Barr, Senator George L. Radcliffe, Dr. J. Hall Pleasants, and Dr. Isaiah Bowman.

Every state, county, city, town, or other public official in Mary-land is *authorized* to deposit in the Hall of Records, any original papers, official books, records, documents, files, newspapers, printed books, or portraits not in use. He is *required* to deposit all records in his custody created before the date of the adoption of the Federal Constitution by Maryland, April 28, 1788. The Hall of Records will furnish for a small fee photostat, typewritten or microfilm copies of any documents in its custody. All the materials at the Hall of Records are available for use by the public in the Search room of the Hall of Records subject to such regulations for their safekeeping as have been adopted by the Hall of Records Commission. Inquiries received by mail will be answered if the research required is con-fined to the use of our extensive indexes; however, no family lines will be traced, nor will any record be evaluated for genealogical purposes.

FOREWORD

As the fourth in its series of publications the Maryland Hall of Records Commission has prepared for students of Maryland history and genealogy this work on colonial land and probate records. Since the county land records and the records of the deputy commissaries general, the county probate officers, are not yet all in Annapolis, it has been thought wise to restrict the scope of these studies to (1) the records which were created by the proprietary and royal land agents and to (2) the archives of the central probate office.

Maryland is fortunate to have preserved such complete land and probate records. Doubtless much credit for this good fortune is due to the fact that the record-making agencies were centralized throughout the colonial period, in St. Mary's City until 1694 and after that in Annapolis. They were ever under the watchful eye of the General Assembly whose proceedings bear witness of the concern felt for those records which protected the property rights of Marylanders. Except for one early incident which accounted for minor losses, these records have escaped the perils of warfare, civil and foreign. They have not been decimated by fire or theft, nor suffered seriously from the other hazards of peace which have caused such grave losses elsewhere. They are all now to be found in the modern fireproof vaults of the Hall of Records building where they receive the best care which a generous State can provide.

All the records considered in these studies are well known to students of Marylandiana. They have been used and cited by specialists for several generations. It is the hope of the authors that this study will widen their usefulness. In the case of the Land records there has never before been a comprehensive list, or catalogue, or finding medium of any kind which might serve to orient the student. It has been fortunate that for the last forty-five years the present Chief Clerk of the Land Office, Mr. Arthur Trader, has been a member of its staff. A generation of students has profited from his interest in, and his knowledge of, these records. Justification for a published list is twofold: the quality of record custodians is certain to vary and students not resident in Annapolis are enabled to prepare themselves in advance for studies here.

Abstracts of the Will records have been published but otherwise none of the probate group has been treated in detail. The several series were accounted for in the Catalogue published by the Hall of Records Commission several years ago, but the usefulness of such a work is, of course, extremely limited.

First drafts of these studies were prepared by the authors several years ago as term papers for the course in Archival Administration offered by American University and the National Archives under the direction of Dr. Ernst Posner. Since that time they have been expanded and thoroughly revised. The authors, Dr. Elisabeth Hartsook, Senior Archival Assistant at the Hall of Records and Gust Skordas, Assistant Archivist, have applied themselves to their difficult and tedious tasks with exceptional perseverance and understanding. Doubtless they will have omitted details or committed minor errors but this is to be expected in pioneering efforts of this kind. That their work is fundamentally sound does not seem subject to doubt.

In addition to the two lists of records the reader will find extremely valuable the historico-legal introductions which precede. A single index for both studies has also been provided.

MORRIS L. RADOFF,

Archivist.

Annapolis,
June 28, 1946.

ACKNOWLEDGEMENTS

The authors wish to express their appreciation to Mr. Roger Thomas, Assistant Archivist at the Hall of Records, for reading the proofs of the study and to Miss Martha Suit, Junior Assistant Librarian, for typing the manuscript. Finally they wish to acknowledge their indebtedness to Dr. Morris L. Radoff, the Archivist, who first suggested the subjects, read the manuscripts and throughout the project lent encouragement and guidance.

ELISABETH HARTSOOK

GUST SKORDAS

LAND OFFICE RECORDS

OF

COLONIAL MARYLAND

By

Elisabeth Hartsook

Whatever the idealistic aims of the founders of Maryland, the problem of making the enterprise pay was a most considerable factor that could not be ignored. Lacking the gold of Mexico or the spices of the Indies, the Lords Baltimore had to make use of the land itself as a source of wealth. The proprietary system, under which Maryland was governed, gave ownership of the soil and complete jurisdiction over it to the Lord Proprietor himself, just as in a medieval fief. Land "bought" was never owned; it was held in fief, or more accurately, in common socage, from the Lord Proprietor. The more of his land that the Lord Proprietor could grant or lease to new settlers the more income he would naturally have from it. Hence the constant campaign to induce people to "come out" to Maryland and take up land.

The basis upon which land was granted was laid down in certain proposals published by the Lord Proprietor, called Conditions of Plantation. Under the first Conditions of Plantation, for example, 2000 acres of land were to be granted to every adventurer taking five men into the new province in the year 1633. All along, too, the Lord Proprietor made special grants, with or without conditions, according to his fancy, to friends and favorites. As things got started, grants were reduced—on the basis of new and successive Conditions of Plantation—and in 1683 title to land was divorced from the condition of importation of new settlers and put on a cash basis—known as purchase or caution money. The amount of the caution money was at first set at 200 pounds of tobacco for every hundred acres. The price was steadily raised, however, until at the time of the overthrow of the proprietary government in 1776 it was five pounds sterling per hundred acres.[1]

Besides caution money payments the Lord Proprietor had three other chief types of land revenue: alienation fines, manor rents and quit rents. An alienation fine was the fee required to be paid to the Lord Proprietor whenever land granted to a tenant was transfer: or conveyed to another person, the amount of the fine usually being equivalent to a year's rent. Quit rents and manor rents differ only in that the former represent the yearly rent paid on freeholds or private land whereas the latter refer to the yearly rent paid on tene-

[1] Clarence P. Gould, *The Land System in Maryland*, 1720-1765, Baltimore, 1913, p. 15.

ments of a manor. A manor was a large grant of land of a thousand acres or more belonging to one individual who rented or leased out parcels of it to tenants. There were about 62 such manors granted to private adventurers in Maryland and about half as many were erected by the Lord Proprietor himself.[2] The manor rents referred to in this study naturally refer only to the manors owned by the Proprietor as rents on the others were collected by the individuals to whom they were granted. The preponderant importance of the quit rents as a source of revenue is readily apparent when one compares average annual income for the years on record from all four types of land revenues. Whereas alienation fines yielded from 130 to 200 pounds sterling each year, manor rents about 1,000 pounds, purchase or caution money payments between 1500 and 2500 pounds, quit rents amounted, on an average, to between five to six thousand pounds.[3] Since the quit rents represented the greatest single item of the Lord Proprietor's income from his colony, it is not surprising that the levying and collection of them was ever a serious issue both for the Lord Proprietor and the Marylanders. The former constantly strove to increase the amount, the latter, to prevent such an increase. The rent began, in 1633, as twenty pounds of wheat per hundred acres. In 1642 it was increased to two shillings for every hundred acres and several years later it was raised to four shillings.[4] In 1671 a duty of twelve pence per hogshead on exported tobacco took the place of normal quit rent (the colony's whole economy at this time was based on the growing and exporting of tobacco) and from 1717 to 1733 a similar law provided a two shilling per hogshead duty to cover all quit rent claims. After 1733 until the Revolution quit rents were again collected normally as before 1671, for the most part at four shillings per hundred acres.[5] Although the total income from manor rents was much less than from freehold rents because there were so many more of the latter, the rent rate for both averaged about the same, the one being higher at one time and the other at another.

---

[2] Donnell MacClure Owings, "Private Manors: An Edited List", p. 307, *Maryland Historical Magazine*, XXXIII, 4, 1938.

[3] Charles A. Barker, *The Background of the Revolution in Maryland*, New Haven, 1940, p. 140.

[4] Gould, p. 33.

[5] Charles A. Barker, "Property Rights in the Provincial System of Maryland," *Journal of Southern History*, II, No. 2, pp. 5-6, 10.

One other, more indirect, source of land revenue for the Proprietor was the reversion of land to him by escheat. All land, under the socage tenure system was liable to revert to the Proprietor if certain conditions—most commonly lack of heirs, treason and non-payment of rent—warranted it. By regranting such land the Lord Proprietor undoubtedly added considerably to his land revenues, if the numerous escheat warrants found in the land records may be taken as an indication.[6] There was always considerable opposition on the part of the colonists to this practice but it continued down to the Revolution.

Although the Lord Proprietor was the one most specifically concerned it must be remembered that he was not the only one to whom land was a matter of primary importance. The soil was the source of livelihood for the people of colonial Maryland and constituted their chief wealth. The mark of landlessness was an unfavorable one and even though landless persons such as leaseholders and overseers made a better living than the poorer freeholders they were left politically powerless and attached to the interest of an upper class. It has been estimated that in 1755 probably more than half of the free whites of Maryland belonged to families of the land-holding class. The great majority of landowners was, of course, made up of the small freeholders, while the great beneficiaries of the land system were those individuals and families whose large holdings gave them power and prestige above the many. This power and prestige was enhanced in the case of many of these individuals by the holding of high offices and the accumulation thereby of considerable additional wealth in the form of fees.

HISTORY OF LAND ADMINISTRATION

In view of the pre-eminent role of land in colonial Maryland it is not surprising that from the beginning the Proprietors took great care of the administration of land affairs and of the keeping of records pertaining thereto.

The earliest evidence of land administration in Maryland comes indirectly through a grant made to Thomas Cornwalleys in 1640 mentioning how in a previous grant "for and in Consideration that our Governor and Comisioners of that our Province of Maryland

---

[6] Gould, pp. 28-29.

did by a Deed under their hand and Seal bearing date of St. Maries
9th May 1634, agree and promise to and with Capt. Henry Fleete
. . . that he should have 4,000 acres of Land."[7] The earliest land
transactions, then, would seem to have been in the hands of the
"Governor and Comisioners." The first official evidence bearing
on land administration is the commission, dated April 15, 1637,
appointing Leonard Calvert as Lieutenant General or Governor of
the province. Among other things Calvert is by this commission
empowered "to pass any Grant under our Said Great Seal . . . All
which Grants Soe to be made . . . and the Said Warrants under our
hand and Seal for the passing thereof, Shall be enrolled by our
Secretary of our said Province, for the time being and not before
. . . Shall be effectual in Law against us, and Shall bind us and
our heirs . . ."[8] This same commission appointed three men as a
Council to the Governor, one of the three (John Lewger) being also
appointed "Secretary and Keeper of the acts and proceedings of
the Governor and Council for the time being, and for the doeing
(i. e. making out) and recording of all grants of land or of offices
within the province," as well for recording generally all matters
necessary.[9] Before the colony began to expand then, land business,
like all other business, was attended to directly by the Governor and
Council and Secretary.

In March 1638/9 an act was passed whereby "no Grant Deed
lease Conveyance or Estate hereafter to be made by the Lord
Proprietarie or his heirs to any person or persons whatsoever . . .
Shall be of any force or validity in law to any intent or purpose
whatsoever untill such grant deed Lease or Conveyance and the
Warrant given or to be given under the hand and Seal of the Lord
Proprietarie of his heirs for the passing and granting the same
shall be enrolled by the Secretary of the Said Province . . ."[10]

In 1641 a new development comes in the establishment of the
office of Surveyor General. This office transcended that of a mere
surveyor and was more like that of the steward of an English
manor. During the first period the incumbent was always a member of the council of state, and was not so much expected to make
surveys himself as to appoint surveyors and control their work and

[7] *Patents*, Liber 1, p. 97; John Kilty, *The Landholder's Assistant and Land Office Guide*, Baltimore, 1808, p. 64.
[8] *Patents*, Liber 1, p. 13.
[9] *Ibid.*, p. 15; Kilty, p. 65.
[10] *Assembly Proceedings*, Liber C & W H, p. 34.

in general to look after all manors, forests, lands, etc. Until the appointment of an Examiner General, 1685, he signed the certificates, and in 1658 his signature began to appear on all grants. In 1671 he was instructed to hold courts of inquiry once a year in each county for examining titles by which land was held, and for ascertaining whether anyone possessed more land than was his due, and what rent ought to be paid; all information thus gained he was to enter in a book, make two copies of the same, send one to the Proprietor and the other to the Receiver General.[11]

The Secretary, in 1670, was given more explicit directions: to prove all rights to land; to inquire after, properly describe, and record all escheats; to enter clearly on record all the proprietary manors and reserves; to prepare a rentroll, diligently to search all concealments of any of the Proprietor's rents, and give notice of any such concealments to the Proprietor and the Governor; to give special attention to procuring the payment of alienation fines, and to have a list of alienations recorded.[12]

Another new office was created sometime between 1671 and 1676 when the Proprietor appointed two Receivers General of his rents and other dues, and authorized them to appoint deputies.[13]

Procedure in obtaining a grant of land in the early years of the colony, then, went something like this. Persons entitled to land came to the Secretary's office to record their entry into the province and consequent right to land under the various Conditions of Plantation. At the same time or perhaps later they demanded warrants of survey—issued by the Governor or the Secretary under his direction—for the corresponding quantities of land. Their claims, once on record, stood to their credit until they chose to use them. Warrants were signed by the Governor and directed to the Surveyor General, who returned certificates of the surveys, under his signature, to the Secretary's office after which, no objection appearing, patents or grants were issued under the great seal signed by the Governor and endorsed by the Secretary and the Surveyor General. The title was then complete and the rights on which it was founded were satisfied and cancelled.[14]

[11] *Archives of Maryland*, V, 94 ff.; Newton D. Mereness, *Maryland as a Proprietary Province*, New York, 1901, p. 59.

[12] *Arch. Md.*, V, 73 ff.; Kilty, p. 59.

[13] *Arch. Md.*, XV, 119 ff.; Kilty, p. 59

[14] *Ibid.*, p. 66.

It is perceived that although land affairs at this period were attended to somewhat confusedly with all other kinds of business in the only office then existing, a framework of the Land Office seems to be already in existence. Kilty is of the opinion that previous to 1680 explicit instructions for the proceedings of the Land Office, and for that purpose only, had not been prescribed—partly because up to that time the government had been generally in the hands of the Proprietor's near relations and partly because up to that time no office had been set aside especially for land. The only clue to such a previous system would seem to lie in a certain "Book of Instructions", no longer in existence, but mentioned in the list of books of records turned over to John Llewellen in 1680.[15] At any rate, Charles, the third Lord Baltimore, is identified with the separate and formal establishment of a Land Office when, in 1680, he for the first time erected an office by that name and gave the charge of it to John Llewellen with the denomination of Register. As such, Llewellen was authorized to take into his care all the "records transcripts, bookes papers and memorandums", to take the probate of rights for land, to issue and sign warrants, and upon return of certificates to draw up patents.[16] The Register, it is seen, now has the powers formerly reserved for the Governor or the Secretary.

Four years after this, Charles, about to make a second visit to England and determined apparently to put land matters on an efficient and dependable basis before leaving, committed the sole management of land affairs to a select council consisting of four members and termed "the land council" or more formally "his Lordships Council for lands specially appointed." At the same time he made out a set of instructions intended to cover all operations of the land office, and from this time the complete and distinct organization of this agency takes its date.[17] The new council was authorized to hear and determine all matters relating to land that were brought before it. Two of its members, the Secretaries of the province, were authorized to issue land warrants, and one of the Secretaries with one of the other members to sign all grants. At this point then, the land business had become thoroughly organized in what was chiefly a private office of the Lord Proprietor, which office held jurisdiction over the keeping of the records, over every-

---

[15] *Warrants*, Liber 3, first page; see p. 77.

[16] *Ibid.*, p. 24.

[17] Kilty, p. 109.

thing pertaining to title to land, and over the collection of the revenue arising thereon.[18]

As a result of the Protestant Revolution of 1688 in England after which Maryland became a crown colony, the Land Office was closed from 1689 to 1694, but its business was to a large extent taken care of nevertheless by Henry Darnall, the proprietor's cousin and his agent. In 1695 Darnall had conferred on him, in as far as the Proprietor was able to do so, all the powers formerly vested in the Land Council[19] and after Darnall's death this power continued to be vested in one person, the Agent, Charles Carroll.

The interval from 1689 to 1715 during which Maryland was a crown colony is especially interesting for the history of the Land Office. The question of the private (i. e. the Lord Proprietor) or public nature of this agency developed into a major issue. Under the royal government the Governor and Council, the Secretary and the Assembly aligned themselves against the Lord Proprietor, his agent and solicitor and assumed many of the rights formerly vested in the Land Council, claiming public rather than private right to settlement of judicial questions relating to title, custody of the record of titles and some control over surveying. About the only rights acknowledged as private and left to the Proprietor were those necessary for securing his legitimate revenue, which from the start the crown had not failed to guarantee him. In effect then, during this period the Land Office was managed by the Royal Governor and Council and more specifically, the Secretary, while the best Lord Baltimore could do was depend on what his agents could achieve in the way of upholding his claims.

None of the subsequent Agents ever brought to their office the power and diligence that Darnall and Carroll had and after the restoration of the Lord Proprietor's rights in 1715, although this office continued, the chief power came to be centered in that of the Land Office Judges newly created at that time. Philemon Lloyd, in 1715, was the first to assume this title. According to the commission received by the second holder of this office the incumbent was constituted "Judge and Register in and of the land office, with full power to hear, judge, and determine in land affairs . . . according to Right, Reason and Good Conscience, and the several instructions and orders which he should from time to time receive from

---

[18] Mereness, p. 60.
[19] Kilty, p. 127-8.

the proprietor relating thereto."[20] Here it is to be observed that the Judge takes over, along with his own title, that of Register. Under the Judges of the Land Office the chief officials were the Surveyor Generals (before the close of the 17th century it had become customary to appoint a Surveyor General for each shore) and the Examiner General. About the only duties of these officers were the appointment of a Deputy Surveyor in each county and the transmission of instructions and warrants to and from these deputies. After 1764 two Judges were appointed for the Land Office and this practice continued until the Revolution.[21]

Such then, was the general organization of land administration in Maryland up to the time of the Revolution. The most striking feature of the development—its constant amplification and diversification— from the small nucleus of the "Governor and Comissioners" to a large office with a number of different departments was to be expected in a new and important agency growing up in a new and important country.

RECORDS IMPLIED IN THE TITLE "COLONIAL LAND OFFICE RECORDS"

Colonial Land Office records are those emanating from the Lord Proprietor's Land Office after its inception in 1680 and kept previous to that in the custody of the authorized director of land affairs. With the exception of assignments they do not witness transactions between two land-holders as conveyances do. They are agreements between an individual and the Lord Proprietor pertaining to initial granting or leasing of land or they are records of rent payments to the Proprietor on his lands. Once an individual received title to land from the Proprietor further transfers (unless the land reverted to the Proprietor through escheat) were no longer recorded in the Land Office, but in either the County Courts or the Provincial Court. Thus a great body of what might at first thought be considered colonial Land Office records—the County and Provincial Court deeds before 1776—does not fall within the scope of this

[20] Kilty, p. 269.
[21] Gould, p. 14.

study. Further, colonial Land Office records discussed here refer only to those in the present custody of the Land Office.[22]

Colonial Land Office records are made up of five different series, according to their present arrangement in the Land Office—*Patents, Warrants, Proprietary Leases, Rent Rolls* and *Debt Books.* The first two series, the *Patents* and *Warrants,* contain not only patents and warrants but also certificates, caveats, proofs of rights, assignments, proclamations of Lord Baltimore, conditions of plantation and all manner of records pertaining to granting of land. These two series actually represent the main body of Land Office records. This is evident from the fact that the various lists of land records made and reported at different times during the colonial period consist of the books of these two series with the Provincial Court land records sometimes included.[23] The reason, of course, that the two series, the *Rent Rolls* and *Debt Books,* do not have the stature of the *Patents* and *Warrants* series is that they were kept as private account books for collecting rent and do not have anything to do with granting or transferring title of land. Proprietary leases fall somewhere between the first group and the second in significance as land records. They record title of a secondary, temporary sort.

THE CHARTER AND CONDITIONS OF PLANTATION

To begin at the very beginning it is necessary to mention the antecedent of all Maryland land records, the charter granting Maryland to Lord Baltimore. The charter granting the territory comprising Maryland had originally been drawn up by George Lord Baltimore, but he dying before the patent was completed, the grant was made on June 20, 1632 to his son Cecilius. By the terms of the charter the territory was to be held in free and common socage from the king of England with a nominal annual rent of two Indian arrows and one-fifth of all gold and silver found. It was made both

[22] Although these records in the present Land Office constitute a complete, definitive body of colonial Land Office records, scattered additional records are to be found at the Maryland Hall of Records, the Maryland Historical Society, in the Johns Hopkins University Papers and in county records. These consist entirely of papers and records of the more private or secondary sort, pertaining to the proprietor's revenue such as duplicates of debt books and rent rolls, lists of manor rents, accounts, alienation lists, etc.

[23] cf. *Arch. Md.,* XX, 192-200; *Provincial Court Land Records,* Liber H. D., pp. 118-124.

alienable and inheritable and the right to grant or lease any of his land to any person to hold the same of him—and not of the king— in fee simple was also given. As to the regulation of military, executive and judicial authority, of all office and title, of the Church and to a large extent, of legislative activity, Lord Baltimore was given almost unrestricted authority, with the crown reserving to itself the right of control in war, trade and commerce. Last but not least, the following provisions were made guaranteeing the rights of the new inhabitants: (1) there should be no ordinance which could take away the right or interest of any person or persons, of, or in member, life, freehold, goods or chattels; (2) all laws and ordinances should be reasonable and, so far as convenient, like the laws and customs of England; (3) the people of Maryland should be entitled to "all the privileges, franchises, and liberties" which other English subjects enjoyed.[24]

The Conditions of Plantation, or terms under which land was granted to new colonists, should be mentioned next. The first of these date from 1633 before the *Ark* and the *Dove* left England. No record of these is extant in Maryland records but secondary sources reveal their existence[25] and they are reproduced in the oldest Conditions of Plantation on record in Maryland, dated 1636 from Portsmouth. By virtue of these two thousand acres are to be granted for every five men (between sixteen and fifty) imported in 1633; one thousand acres for every five men imported in 1634 or since; for lesser numbers one hundred acres for each man or woman and fifty acres for each child; each tract of 1000, 2000 or 3000 acres to be erected into a manor under such name as the adventurer may choose; rents to average twenty pounds of wheat per hundred acres annually.[26] After this three subsequent Conditions of Plantation were published, all from London, in 1641, 1648 and 1649. All were finally supplanted by the new 1683 ruling governing conditions of plantation by which all granting of land was put on a money payment basis. In this same category various letters and proclamations by the Lord Proprietor may be mentioned. While Lord Baltimore was in England he often sent commissions and letters of instruction to the Governor concerning land affairs. The Governor in turn would

---

[24] Mereness, pp. 7-9.

[25] *Narratives of Early Maryland* 1633-1684, edited by Clayton Colman Hall, New York, 1910.

[26] *Patents*, Liber 4, p. 61, 62.

issue proclamations setting forth the instructions which often were exhortations to colonists to prove land rights before a certain date, extra instructions in regard to procedure with manors, more specific directions as to who should be allowed to take up grants and where, and so on. These are to be found recorded in the early *Patents* or in the *Council Proceedings* for that period.

CONTENTS OF PATENTS, WARRANTS AND PROPRIETARY LEASES SERIES

The first type of Maryland land record proper to be found is the record of entry. These include entry records of people who came in 1633, but the earliest date of recording is not till a few years later. The earliest ones, as may be observed on the first pages of Liber I of the *Patents,* are bare reports of arrival in the colony, such as:

> Came into the Province 28th November 1637 in the ship called the Unity of the Isle of Wight—Mr. John Lewger, who transported his wife, his son John aged 9 years, Martha Williamson, Ann Pike, and Mary Whitehead, Maid Servants, Benjamine Cobby, Phillip Linnis, Thomas Furston, and a Boy Robert Serle aged 12 years.

This type of entry was a little too simple because it did not state the exact number of persons transported. Since land was granted according to the number of persons brought in the entries had to be more specific, as appears a little further on in the record:

> Entered by John Lewger, Secretary, brought into the Province in the year 1637, John Lewger, senior, Ann his wife, John Lewger, Jr. aged 9 years—Martha Williamson, Ann Pike, Mary Whitehead maid servants Benjamin Cobby &c. the same persons mentioned in the entry of arrivals, and others to the number of 22.

The latter type of entry is supposed to be an official admission or proof of the claims of the various parties to land proportionate to the number of persons brought in by them. At a later date, 1662, these entry records were ordered to be made under oath.[27] They came to be called "proofs of rights" and in their definitive form read:

> 28 July 1671   Came John Brown of St. Mary's County and proved his Right to fifty Acres of Land it being due to him for

---

[27] Kilty, p. 76; *Council Book* HH, p. 148.

transporting himself out of Virginie into this province to
inhabite.[28]

The second type of record that appears goes by the name of a
demand. This is simply a demand on the part of the arrival for a
warrant of survey for the amount of land coming to him. These
demands might be grounded upon Conditions of Plantation as:

> 4th April 1643. Nathaniel Orchard demandeth 100 acres of
> land due by Conditions of Plantation for transporting himself
> into the Province in the year 1640.[29]

or upon special warrants granted by Lord Baltimore under whatever terms he chose to impose.

The next logical instrument is the warrant itself. This is an official precept issued by the Governor or by the Secretary, and later
by the Registers and various others empowered thereto, to the
Surveyor, directing him to lay out and survey the requisite amount
of land for the claimant and to return a certificate of his survey.
For example:

> 4th March 1641—Lay out for John Cockshut, fiftie acres of
> Land upon the Hill next beyond the hill Creek called St.
> Joseph's Hill and certifie the bounds thereof unto our Secretary
> without delay.[30]

In addition to the foregoing "common warrant" there was also the
"special warrant" issued or directed to be issued by Lord Baltimore
himself with whatever conditions he might prescribe. Included in
this category would be gifts, grants, orders, and so on. For example,
James Lindsey and Richard Willan were given a special warrant
for a grant of the manor of Snow Hill as a reward for service
rendered by them during Ingle's insurrection.[31] Sometimes too, con-
ditional warrants were granted—warrants issued on an agreement
to make rights good within a specified time. Similarly, later on
when money payments took the place of entry rights, warrants were
occasionally granted on credit.

After the warrant had been obtained the certificate of survey was
the record to be procured next. It was to follow the warrant within
some prescribed time, at this time still arbitrary, but usually aver-

---

[28] *Patents*, Liber 15, p. 127.
[29] *Ibid.*, Liber 4, p. 22.
[30] *Ibid.*, Liber 4, p. 58.
[31] *Ibid.*, Liber 3, p. 410.

aging six months. When the survey had been completed it was signed by the Surveyor General who returned it to the Secretary's office. A certificate of survey dated Dec. 4, 1639 in Liber 1 of *Patents* reads:

> Laid out for Mr. William Lewis one neck of land lying upon the northern side of St. Inigoes Creek and bounding on the west with St. Andrew's Creek; on the east with the freehold of St. Maries Hill, and on the north with the town land of Robert Clerk as it is distinguished by marked trees containing thirty acres or thereabouts.
>
> JOHN LEWGER (Surveyor)

When the foregoing records had all been completed and if no objections were forthcoming the patent itself was granted under the great seal, signed by the Governor and endorsed by the Secretary and the Surveyor General. The patent or grant[32] was of the nature of a deed, and gave the consideration for which the grant was made, the description of the grant as found in the certificate of survey and the conditions of tenure.[33] The following is an example of a patent:

> Caecilius &c: To all persons to whom these presents shall come greeting in our Lord God Everlasting. Know yee that we for and inconsideration that George Peake of this province planter, hath due unto him Three hundred Acres of Land for the transportation of Severall persons into this Province here to inhabitt as appears upon record. And upon such conditions and terms as are Expressed in our conditions of plantation of our Province of Maryland under our greater Seal at Armes bearing date at London the Second day of July in the Year of our Lord God One Thousand Six hundred forty nine with such alteration as in them is made by our declaration bearing date the twenty Sixth day of August One Thousand Six hundred fifty one and remaining upon record in our sd Province of Maryland Do hereby grant unto him the sd George Peake a Parcell of Land (called Peake Marsh) lying in Talbotts County on the North side of Choptanck River. . . . To have and to hold the same unto him the said George Peake his heirs and assigns forever To be holden of us and our heirs, as of our Mannor of Baltemore in free and common Soccage by fealty only for all manner of Services Yeilding and Paying therefore yearly unto us and our heirs at our receipt at Saint Maries at the two most

---

[32] These two terms are used interchangeably though the latter usually refers to what is granted and the former to the record of it.

[33] Mereness, p. 51.

usuall feasts in the year. . . . by even and equall Portions the
Rent of Six Shillings Sterling. . . . or the full value thereof in
such comodities as we. . . . shall accept in discharge thereof . . .
Given at Saint Maries under our great Seal of our sd Province
of Maryland the Six and twentieth day of September in the
three and thirtieth Year of our dominion over our sd Province
of Maryland Annoq Domi One Thousand Six hundred Sixty
three Wittness our dear Son and heir Charles Calvert Esq our
Lieut. Generall of our sd Province of Maryland.[34]

The foregoing represent the chief basic types of land records.
There are, however, many others that developed out of these primary
ones or are variations of them. One of the early developments is the
assignment or transfer of rights, warrants, certificates and even of
patents from one person to another. For a while—before the law
put a stop to it—patents were transferred conveying complete title
in land from one person to another without a deed indented or the
other ordinary formalities. The reverse side of the patent was
simply endorsed and sometimes the same patent might be endorsed
with several successive assignments.[35] Warrants and certificates
were regularly assigned by making and acknowledging the assignment before the Secretary and having him enter it on records. The
assignments of rights to land were so numerous as to lead Kilty to
the belief that there must have been books subsidiary to those of
general record for the purpose of entering the rights in a short form
in succession as they were exhibited.[36] If it is borne in mind that
with the exception of tobacco, land rights constituted almost the
only medium of exchange among the early colonists, this practice
of assignment is the more readily understandable.

Two main types of warrants have already been observed but there
are three or four other important types that should be mentioned,
namely, warrants of resurvey and three variations thereof—escheat,
proclamation, and surplus warrants. Warrants of resurvey were
the natural outgrowth of incorrect original surveys and the desire
for precise information as to the boundaries of one's land. All during
the proprietary period these warrants were not generally granted as
a matter of right and were preceded by petitions stating the object
of the application for resurvey. This fact, plus the great number
of resurvey warrants upon the records, gives an indication of their

[34] *Patents*, Liber 8, p. 72.
[35] Kilty, p. 211.
[36] *Ibid.*, pp. 77-8.

real nature and importance—the extension and improvement of one's land. Though there were theoretical restrictions, the resurvey warrant was permitted to serve a variety of advantageous purposes such as the excluding of bad and taking in of better lands, obtaining allowance for actual deficiency, for water comprehended in the first survey or ground subsequently washed away, etc.[37]

Escheat warrants also present an enormous figure on the records, partly no doubt, for the same reason as the resurvey warrants. The practice of escheat—whereby land escheated or reverted to the Lord Proprietor—was an inheritance from the feudal system of land tenure. In practice a man might present a petition to the land authorities stating that his neighbor had died without heirs and requesting a decision as to whether the land was liable to escheat or not. If the decision of the investigating jury confirmed the escheat-ability of the land, the petitioner then applied for an escheat warrant and was usually given preference over others as the "discoverer", in obtaining the warrant. (Since escheats were not easily traceable by the land officers, it was the policy to give some premium to discoverers).[38] This sort of warrant brought with it the same privileges already mentioned in connection with resurvey warrants. The type did not occur frequently before the last quarter of the 17th century but increased greatly after that and continued to be issued down to the Revolution. In the latter part of the proprietary period, however, proclamation warrants came to supersede escheat warrants to a considerable extent especially in cases of land reverting for reasons other than lack of heirs. The warrants in question are founded upon three successive proclamations of Charles, Lord Baltimore, whereby persons who had made surveys comprehending vacant or escheat land, and who neglected to pay or compound therefor, and to take out their patents within a limited time, were subjected to the loss of all the rights derived from such surveys; the lands becoming by means of such omission liable to be taken by the first discoverer, under new warrants to be obtained for that purpose.[39]

Surplus warrants are unique in that they were issued for a very short period only—between 1735 and 1738. They represent an attempt on the part of the Lord Proprietor to recover some of the excess of land included with the bounds of surveys beyond the

---

[37] *Ibid.*, p. 134-5.
[38] *Ibid.*, p. 174.
[39] *Ibid.*, p. 186-7.

quantities intended and declared to be granted. Various attempts were made, by proclamations, to get people to resurvey their land and either give up or purchase their surplus. Results being negligible the Proprietor in 1733 issued another proclamation giving to the first discoverers the privilege of making resurveys on the lands of others and appropriating to themselves the surplusage. The warrants arising therefrom caused such confusion and dissatisfaction however that they were soon discontinued, and further efforts on the part of the Lord Proprietor to recover surplus lands met with increasingly fruitless results.[40]

Another widely used instrument was the caveat. This is the name given to the formal complaint, protesting issuance of patent, which a person lodged with the Governor or Secretary or other proper authority in the Land Office whenever such a person discovered that the survey or warrant of another was going to interfere with his rights. After the complaint had been formally entered the matter was brought to a hearing and determined on "principles of equity and good conscience" by the chief authority of the Land Office. An irregular use of caveats developed during the years of the Cromwell protectorate when they were entered in the Land Office for lands which individuals wanted to secure for themselves till some future time when they could have it surveyed. The practice was abolished after the Restoration of Charles II.[41]

Manor leases are one other form of record to be mentioned. The proprietary manors made up a huge amount of land and from the very beginning were offered to be leased to tenants in small holdings. Probably because of the abundance of cheap land that could be privately owned, these leases were not taken up to any great extent during the seventeenth century. After the restoration of proprietary rights when good vacant land was beginning to become scarce the manor leasing flourished and became a source of considerable income to the Proprietor. Rent on these leases in the earlier part of the eighteenth century was almost uniformly ten shillings per hundred acres, but as the manors became more developed and increased in value rents were pushed up so that in 1755 rents in Anne Arundel Manor were increased to five pounds sterling per hundred acres. In addition to rents, there were often provisions in the leases requiring

---

[40] *Ibid.*, p. 197-8.
[41] *Ibid.*, p. 215.

the erection of dwellings and the planting of fruit trees, etc. Terms of the leases ran from five to twenty-one years or for three lives, with a strong tendency to favor three lives and twenty-one years, the Proprietor generally refusing to grant leases for any longer terms. When manor land was leased, the steward in charge of the manor ran the lines of the tenement, made out a certificate, and drew a lease in duplicate. These were sent to the agent, who, if he approved, signed the leases himself, secured the Governor's signature, and returned one of the duplicates to the steward to be delivered to the tenant. Each steward was supposed to keep a roll on which all leases were entered and which showed the amounts of rent due. According to this roll the rents were collected and turned over to the agent.[42]

PATENTS, WARRANTS AND PROPRIETARY LEASES AS ARCHIVAL SERIES

At the beginning, of course, the land records were not divided into series; they were not even segregated and kept as one series. For the first few years land records, Court Proceedings, Assembly Proceedings and every kind of business, were entered into one book in the order of their occurrence, and kept in the office of the Secretary of the province. Because of this circumstance the first volumes of the Land Office records have preserved in copied form valuable records and proceedings otherwise lost. This situation holds true only of the very first volumes, however, for almost immediately separate land records began to be kept. In fact, in Liber A B & H of the *Patents* series we have the case of a volume made up of land records extracted from among the Court Proceedings and other business of Libers A, F and H and put into one convenient volume of just land records.

After the separate set of records for land was established it was still quite a while before any separation of the different types of land records into series took place. Assignments, entry rights, patents, warrants, certificates were all entered just as they came into the office. The first step towards an orderly organization was the putting of little batches of certificates, of warrants, of patents, together. This idea gradually developed and in 1680, just after the

---

[42] Gould, p. 91-97.

Land Office was first organized and the numerous reforms of the second Lord Baltimore put into effect, separate volumes came to be devoted to patents, to warrants, and to certificates and assignments. Things did not immediately proceed quite this definitely for there was a relapse for a short time, possibly due to the unsettlement preceding the Revolution of 1688. It is safe to say, however, that from 1700 on the separation of patents, certificates and warrants was definite and steadily perfected itself. Actually, instead of two series there are three, for though patents and certificates are included in the same series, each is kept in different volumes.

The *Patents* series, from 1634 to 1777, contains one hundred and thirty-three volumes of which some sixty-nine contain patents only, some thirty-eight contain certificates and assignments only and the remainder — all belonging to the earliest period — contain land records of all types. The first four books of the *Patents* series, as has already been suggested and as may be noted in the appended list, contain not only land records of all types but also Court Proceedings, proclamations, Assembly Proceedings and other kinds of business of the province. With Liber 4, or AB&H as it is also called, the entries become confined to land records and from Liber 25 on (or about the year 1680) patents and certificates begin to be kept separately.

The *Warrants* series contains forty-two volumes, the earliest dating from 1661. Actually the first two volumes of the series contain land records of all types (they are also both duplicated in the *Patents* series)[43] and the second two contain primarily the proceedings of the Land Council, so that the *Warrants* series proper might be considered to begin with the fifth volume of the series—or around 1680 when warrants first began to be kept separately from other land records.

As had already been noted, these records were kept in the Secretary's office in the early day of the province. In 1680, with the establishment of the Land Office and the creation of the office of Register of the Land Office, the Register became the custodian of them. During the royal government period the controversy over the public or private nature of the land records resulted as we have seen in the patents, warrants and all records relating to title

---

[43] *Warrants* Liber 1 is the equivalent of *Patents* Libers 6 and 7, and *Warrants* Liber 2 is a photocopy of a transcript of *Patents* Liber 0.

being adjudged public and hence left in the custody of the Royal Secretary rather than with the Proprietor's Agent. At the end of the royal period the Register again resumed custody and kept it throughout the remainder of the colonial period.

The records of these two important series have on the whole been preserved remarkably well. On not a few occasions, from the seventeenth century on, there was agitation and subsequent legislative action in the interests of their preservation. With the lists of land records as they exist today I have included a list of the land records as they existed in 1680 (a list identical, except for later additions, to another list compiled in 1694).[44] Only four of the thirty books of the 1680 list are missing today and one of them, Liber D, is not a land record but a book of instructions pertaining to land matters and another, Liber RM, is a land record of a restricted type. It deals with lands in what is now Delaware, and may possibly be in existence in that state. The other two missing volumes are Liber I&K "Burles 2 Bookes of Rights from 1649 to 1657", and Liber P "Booke of Rights & Warrants 1660" which appears to be missing already on the 1694 list.[45]

PROPRIETARY LEASES

The *Proprietary Leases* series consists of just three volumes. All the leases, as the title implies, are leases between the Lord Proprietor (represented by his agent) and individuals who rented lands on his manors or reserves. It appears that though some leases were recorded in county land records, as a whole they were not recorded regularly in a separate volume series the way patents and other instruments were. Instead they were made out in duplicate and the lessee and the agent each received a copy. The agent was to keep these, but apparently he lacked a methodical system in so doing. In 1757 Governor Sharpe complains to the proprietor of "the Neglect of those who have heretofore had the Care & Management of these Lands None of whom have recorded or kept Copies of the Leases that they granted, & as many Tenants have lost their leases & know not how their Lands are situated or bounded."[46] Later the same year he writes in another letter to Lord Baltimore: ". . . The Steward

---

[44] cf. p. 77.

[45] *Arch. Md.*, XX, 192-200.

[46] *Ibid.*, VI, 322-523.

or Agent should I think keep a Book by way of Record for every mannour wherein all Leases for or Agreements concerning Parcells of such Mannour should be duly entered & also a proper and particular Description of every Tract or parcell that should be leased or Tenanted . . ."[47] In his 1761 instructions for setting up the Board of Revenue, Lord Baltimore specifically provided for proper custody of his leases:

> After the said Office shall be fitted up, you are to lodge therein all Counterparts of Leases (which have been granted for any Lands of mine) that are now in your Possession, and as often as our Lieutenant Governor, and you, shall for the future grant any Leases for my Manor or Reserved Lands, you shall Lodge the Counterparts thereof in the said Office, placing and titling them in such Methodical manner as that Recourse may easily be had thereto on all Occasions.[48]

The apparent neglect in keeping the proprietary leases was doubtless partly due to the fact that in the early days there were not many leases held because there was so much freehold land available. Further, during the royal period the manors seem to have been much neglected and the whole system of proprietary leasing allowed to go to pieces. Under the circumstances it is not difficult to understand that orderly preservation of the leases did not prevail. After the royal period, the Proprietor's interest in the manors revived, there was a considerable increase in the number of tenants and more efficient methods of supervising the manors were adopted. In fact manor rents were at their peak and showed promise of further increase at the time when Lord Baltimore decided to sell all his manors in 1764. By far the great majority of leases in this series are dated after 1730.

Although, as we have seen, Governor Sharpe in 1756 was advocating recording of the leases, his plan was apparently never carried out by the proprietary government. The three volumes of leases as we have them were not compiled till almost a century later, when George G. Brewer, Register of the Land Office from 1827 to 1851, seems to have arranged and recorded them.[49] The first two volumes

---

[47] *Ibid.*, IX, 62.
[48] *Ibid.*, XXXII, 391.
[49] In *Proprietary Leases*, Liber B. pp. 595 and 601 certain footnotes or notations concerning endorsements on leases are to be found. They are signed "Geo. G. Brewer Reg. Land Office" and there is no doubt, from the handwriting and arrangement on the page, that they were written at the time the leases were copied.

consist entirely of leases of lands in Baltimore County and the third volume contains leases from Anne Arundel, Cecil, Kent, Queen Anne's, Dorchester, St. Mary's, Charles, Somerset, Worcester, and Prince George's counties. Entries of leases are alphabetical by name of lease-holder except in the third volume where this order is not always maintained. Dates of the leases range from 1707 to 1771, with the majority falling in the forties and fifties.

At one time there were also plats to the Proprietor's manors. Governor Sharpe in a letter to Lord Baltimore in 1757 speaks of having "entered in a Book Platts of most of your Ldps Mannours in the different parts of the Province".[50] That book may exist somewhere among the Calvert family papers. The Land Office has about a dozen individual manor plats in its custody at the present time.

RENT ROLLS AND DEBT BOOKS SERIES

The two remaining series of Land Office records, the *Rent Rolls* and *Debt Books* are considerably different from the records of the *Patents* and *Warrants* series. In a sense they are just the Lord Proprietor's account books and not Land Office records at all. In fact the dispute over the public or private nature of land records during the royal period definitely established the rent rolls and debt books as private records. However, since all land records were looked upon as more or less private prior to this dispute and the Land Office considered a private matter by the Proprietor himself, it is plain that before the royal period rent rolls and debt books were considered Land Office records. Furthermore, while the Proprietor's personal hold on land affairs was much weakened during the royal period it was immediately revived when his proprietary rights were restored in 1715. Forceful efficiency measures on his part tended to bring land and revenue matters back under the old single rein, as witness the fact that in 1760 the Proprietor "proposed that part of that Office [the Land Office] shall be a Repository for all the Farm Contracts from the Rent Roll Keepers . . . And in that Office to be Deposited the Leases of all Mannour Lands & of all other Rights payable to the Ld Proprietor . . ."[51] Likewise in 1770-1771 we find the question of the private or public nature of

---

[50] *Arch. Md.*, VI, 522.

[51] *Ibid.*, IX, 403.

the Land Office causing a great stir again.[52] So, although rent rolls and debt books came more and more to be classified among the Proprietor's revenue records— in 1760 the Proprietor wrote that he "thinks it proper that the Rent Roll Keepers place should belong to the Office of the Receivers General"[53]—the connection between the revenue system and operations of the Land Office was nevertheless so close as to make it almost impossible to separate the two completely from each other. Thus it seems that while it is safe to call rent rolls and debt books private in contrast to patents and warrants it is not permissible to exclude them as non-Land Office records.

The rent rolls and debt books are the books in which the Lord Proprietor kept track of the rents due him. Each piece of land granted to a person was subject to a yearly rent according to the terms in the patent. The original owner might die and his son inherit; in such a case the son then paid the rent. If a man sold his land the new owner was then to pay the rent. In any case the Lord Proprietor was to continue receiving his annual rent on every tract of land granted. A rent roll consists of entries of each tract of land patented plus the name of the person for whom it was originally surveyed, the present owner and the acreage and rent. Alienations, or subsequent sales and leases of the piece of land, are also included. A debt book consists of a list of persons owning land with the names and rents of each tract he owns all listed in one place under his name. In other words debt-book entries are by the name of the owner whereas rent-roll entries are by the name of tracts of land. They plainly represent a more efficient method of collecting rents—a corollary and later refinement of rent rolls. Since debt books do not appear until a hundred years after the rent rolls and are more or less just a modification of them, this series will necessarily receive subordinate treatment. Rent rolls and debt books as we have them are always made out by counties but it is to be assumed that in the very earliest days a common rent roll was kept for all tracts of land.

The first rent roll of the series dates from the year 1659 but, as has just been suggested, there were probably earlier ones in one form or another. Keeping wills, patents and court proceedings all in the same volume was all very well, but to depend on such a

---

[52] *Lower House Journal*, November 22, 1771; Mereness, pp. 71-75.
[53] *Arch. Md.*, IX, 404.

helter-skelter arrangement for looking up and computing the rents —even in those first twenty years or so of the colony—would have been highly inefficient to say the least. At this early period the preparation and keeping of rent rolls were in the hands of the Secretary of the province and the Surveyor General.[54] With the creation of the office of Receiver General, another official took a hand in the compiling of the rent rolls, for in 1678 there was a proclamation of the Proprietor ordering recording of alienations "in order that the Secretary and the Receiver General might be able to make a complete rent roll."[55] Indeed, sometime before 1676 the Proprietor appointed two Receivers General of his rents and other dues and authorized them to appoint deputies.[56] From an early date whoever was in charge of rent rolls was assisted by the sheriffs who made the collections locally and forwarded them. A commission to the sheriffs from the governor in 1671 reads:

> . . . These are therefore in the name of his said Lordship to will and Command you that you Cause a true and perfect Rent Roll to be made of all and singular the Lands in your County and in whose possession they now are & distinguish them by Debtor and Creditor and give them Credit that have paid and if they have not paid then to each piece of Land say (over against it) not paid and if there be no distress you shall likewise incert so over against the said Land you shall make a full Inquiry into all and singular the premises that you may be the better Enabled to make a Certain and Perfect Rent Roll which Rent Roll shall begin with the first Seated hundred in your County and so successively & the said Rent Roll and a true Copy thereof attested under your hand that you personally bring with you into the City of Saint Marys the first day of October next ensuing the date hereof and therein exhibite unto my self and Council who will be God willing then there to make a full Examination into his Lordships Rents and also give you such further Orders Instructions and directions touching both that and other his Lordships Affairs as to us shall seem expedient. . . .[57]

From 1689 to 1715 Maryland became a royal colony and the Proprietor had continually to contend for his rights in land affairs and the custody of the land records. Between 1689 and 1694 the Land

---

[54] *Arch. Md.*, V, 94 ff.; Mereness, p. 59.

[55] *Arch. Md.*, XV, pp. 159, 160; Mereness, p. 60.

[56] *Arch. Md.*, XV, p. 119 ff.; Mereness, p. 59.

[57] *Proceedings of the Council of Maryland*, 1667-75, p. 70; *Arch. Md.*, V, 91.

Office was closed. During this whole period a special land agent appointed by the Proprietor (he had previously been the Receiver General) represented and championed the latter in all matters pertaining to land and it was he who had charge of the rent rolls at this time. The agent continued to be Receiver General in charge of rent rolls after the restoration of Lord Baltimore's rights in 1715 but since the tobacco tax took the place of quit rents during the years between 1717 and 1733 rent rolls were not as important during these years and not carefully kept. Still, the Proprietor attempted to keep his records straight in this respect. In 1722 he wrote to his agent Nicholas Lowe:

> ... You are to acquaint Mr. James Carroll that I would have him make out my Rent Roll according to my late Directions to him, In the doing whereof I desire him to Consult with you and Transmit it forthwith to me. ...[58]

and in 1724 Lord Baltimore granted Carroll fifty-eight hundred acres of land with the provision "But he is to pay me no fine, it being a reward bestowed on him (in addition to the 4,200 acres formerly given him) for his labor and pains in keeping and making out my rent rolls ..."[59]

In 1733, with the resumption of the payment of quit rents, the Proprietor issued a great many new instructions designed to facilitate collection. The Governor and the Agent were to appoint two general rent-roll keepers, one for each shore. The rents were to be collected by deputy receivers in each county or by quit rent farmers who were to return them annually to the rent roll keeper of their respective shores. The sheriff often served as deputy receiver, if that method was used. The farmer on the other hand did not always collect by counties, sometimes collecting in just a part of a county, or sometimes contracting to collect in two or three counties. The Eastern Shore debt books date from this period.

The Proprietor made a still more definite and far-reaching attempt to increase the efficiency of quit rent collection when he established the Board of Revenue in 1766 and gave it highest control over all matters pertaining to his revenues. It had jurisdiction over every class of officers concerned in the management or collection of his

[58] *Arch. Md.*, XXXVIII, 432.
[59] *Warrants*, Liber 9, f. 420; Kilty, p. 228-229.

revenues, the Commissary General, Clerks of the provincial and county courts, the Attorney General, Sheriffs, Examiner, and Naval Officers as well as those having to do with the collection of quit rents. Since this system represents the highest point of development in the keeping of rent rolls and debt books it may be well to observe it in some detail in Kilty's admirable analysis:

... There was a general rent roll keeper for each shore, whose duty it was by a certain day in every year to make out, sign, and deliver, the necessary debt books to the farmers or receivers of the quit rents in each county of their respective shores. In order that the rent rolls might be complete the judges of the land office were bound to return to the keepers, annually a list of all the lands patented within the twelve months immediately preceding. Returns were also to be made to them by the commissary general, and register of the prerogative office, of all alterations in the possession and title of lands, whether by descent or devise, and the clerks of the provincial and county courts were to make return of all alienations of land by them recorded within the year, the substance of which returns was to be added to. the former entries:—the debt books contained the names of all persons that possessed land within the counties for which they were respectively made, and the name and quantity of every parcel of land, under what rent held, and what quit rents each tenant was annually to pay for his land whether he might hold one or more tracts:—the gross amount of those debt books was to be reported by the keepers to the proprietary's agent, and new and complete copies of the rentall were to be prepared by them, and lodged with the clerk of the revenue office.

The receivers were to return back, within a stated time, annually, the debt books received by them for the preceding year, accompanied by such observations as might tend to make the rent rolls more perfect, and with a probate that no quit rents had been received which were not there stated; that they know of no tracts *patented, improved,* or *occupied,* but what were there entered, and that the persons employed by them to assist in the collection had taken a similar oath.

The rent roll keeper upon thus receiving back the debt books, stated an account for each receiver, debiting him with the gross amount of the debt book, and crediting him with all warranted allowances, any disputes concerning which were to be submitted to the revenue board, and distinct copies of these accounts were to be furnished to the agent, and to the board.

The receivers were authorized to sue or distrain in his lordship's name or their own. — On blank leaves, to be left in the debt books, they were to note alienations happening after the receipt of those books, and errors and defects in the books themselves;—to enter lands not duly charged;—to demand arrears of rent, and to consider the discovery of such arrears, a part of their duty.

In consideration that the rents were payable half yearly by the tenants, the receivers were required to make a payment of one third directly after their first receipts, and to make before the close of the year a full and complete settlement with the rent roll keeper;—immediately after such settlement, to produce to the receiver general the debt books, examined by the keeper, together with the settled account, signed, and pay the remaining two thirds of the collections, ten per cent being allowed for their services;—they were to have free access to all offices, with liberty to take copies or extracts without fee, unless the attestation of the officer was required, and were to transfer such copies to their successors: in case of disputes with the tenants, they were to apply to the attorney general or his deputies for advice and assistance: they were in all things to observe the instructions of the board of revenue, and to return all books and papers in their charge to that board when called for.[60]

It is clear that the Board of Revenue exercised a most effective control over the collection and book-keeping of the Proprietor's quit rents. Such then, was the final development in the keeping of rent rolls and debt books, for the Board of Revenue continued to operate till the Revolution.

The rent rolls in the present Land Office appear to be a complete, continuous series from 1639 to 1776 and are frequently so listed, but this is not exactly the case. The first book of the series—Liber 0—contains the rent rolls of St. Mary's, Charles, Calvert and Kent counties, four volumes, each with individual paging bound together into one single re-paginated volume. Entries go up to but not beyond 1659 and at the end of the Charles and Kent County rent rolls is found the notation "Extrahitur ex Record" with the signature "Phillip Calvert Sec." Calvert was Secretary between 1656 and 1660 so it seems permissible to assign 1659 as the definite date of Liber 0. This book is unique in the series, having much more detailed entries and a different form from all the other volumes in addition to a definite date of completion, 1659. It is definitely an authentic, contemporary rent roll whereas it is difficult to date any of the other rent rolls until much later. Its uniqueness in this series

---

[60] *Arch. Md.*, XXXII, 391 *et seq.*; Kilty, pp. 258-260.

is explained by the fact that it is a photocopy, recently made, of original rent rolls in the possession of the Maryland Historical Society. Owing partly to the private aspect of rent rolls and debt books and partly to the custom of making duplicate copies of them, a considerable number of these are to be found in private collections, particularly the Calvert Papers.

As for the rest of the series, the year 1734 seems to mark a definite point. All entries previous to 1734 are noted in Eastern Shore rent rolls as being in the "Old Rent Roll" and subsequent additional rent rolls are regularly entered each year thereafter. All the entries in the "Old Rent Roll" appear to have been copied at one time, i.e., there is no complete rent roll for an earlier date such as the 1659 one in Liber 0. There *were* other original rent rolls previous to 1734, because some are extant in private collections. The fact that they, like the original of Liber 0, do not exist in such form in the *Rent Roll* series in the Land Office today is not too difficult to explain. It has already been noted that during the controversy over land records while Maryland was a royal colony it was decided that whereas patents, warrants, certificates, etc. were a matter of public concern and therefore to be kept by the royal government and open to the public, rent rolls were the private business of the Proprietor. As such then, rent rolls were kept by the Proprietor's agent and did not become public records in the sense that patents, etc. recorded at that time did. A second fact to be taken into account is that between 1717 and 1733 a law provided for payment of a tobacco tax on every hogshead of tobacco shipped out of the province to take the place of payment of quit rents. It is not strange that during this period, as Mereness points out, the rent rolls fell into confusion by disuse.[61] A third consideration, and a most likely one it seems to me, is that the rent rolls as the Land Office has them (with the exception of Liber 0) were compiled in 1733 and thereafter, but were based on earlier rent rolls then in existence. The year 1733 marked the end of the system of paying tobacco tax in lieu of quit rents and with the re-establishment of the quit rent system the proprietor took steps to improve the rent collection system. What more logical than the compiling of fresh new rent rolls to resume the system with, especially if recent ones had been incomplete and ill-kept?

---

[61] Mereness, p. 65.

After 1734 the *Rent Rolls* series seems to proceed in continuous, complete fashion, especially in the Eastern Shore rolls. Western Shore rent rolls after 1734 were not kept in a uniform, orderly fashion each year until many years later. There, every few years or so each county seemed to make up a rent roll which would then be known as the "Rent Roll of 1758" or the "Rent Roll of 1762", in which all entries were brought up to date since the last rent roll. But the years varied in different counties and it is impossible to say that the series is complete even though all dates seem to be included, with the exception of Calvert and St. Mary's Counties for which no entries between 1769 and 1775 are to be found. In 1768 the Board of Revenue apparently established a more rigid system and a regular annual additional rent roll was made for each county, as had been done in Eastern Shore counties ever since 1734.

The *Debt Book* series, as has been pointed out, goes back to 1733 for the Eastern Shore counties. Western Shore debt books in the Land Office series begin in 1753, but debt books for the year 1750 are to be found in the Calvert Papers for five Western Shore counties. Each debt book, in its present make-up, consists of from two to eight small volumes bound together into one. This series appears to have been very imperfectly preserved. Over a third of the small annual volumes are missing, mostly in Eastern Shore counties. Only for Charles and St. Mary's counties has the whole series been preserved completely, and since these are both Western Shore counties that means they only date from 1753. Like the rent rolls the debt books were made out in duplicate.

Apropos of the missing debt books and rent rolls mentioned in the foregoing paragraphs, it would seem that the Land Office in the colonial period had a great many more books and papers relating to quit rents which are no longer to be found. This is primarily due, no doubt, to the fact that they were private revenue papers of the Proprietor rather than public records, and secondarily, to the fact that they were for the most part papers rather than volumes. "A List of Books and Papers Relating to the Right Honourable the Lord Proprietarys Rent Rolls of the Eastern Shore received from Col. Edward Tilghman Nov. 13, 1756"[62] enumerates in addition to rent rolls and debt books, a great number of alienation lists, lists of de-

---

[62] A miscellaneous volume at the Hall of Records.

vises, observations and queries about land, accounts, instructions, abstracts of land records, lists of resurveys, escheats, insolvencies, disclaimers and arrears. With the exception of the debt books and rent rolls and a small collection of papers at the Maryland Hall of Records, these have not been preserved by the Land Office.

The above comprehensive list of books and papers relating to rent rolls on the Eastern Shore suggests that a comparison of Eastern and Western Shore methods of land administration might be a fruitful one. It seems to me that this list is indicative of a highly developed efficiency in keeping the records that is not matched on the Western Shore. It will be remembered that from an early date there were two Receivers General, one for each shore, and that in 1733 a rent-roll keeper was specifically appointed for each shore. Apparently each had considerable latitude in the methods used for collecting quit rents and keeping rent rolls. Mention has already been made of the regularity of additional rent roll entries in Eastern Shore rent rolls after 1733 in contrast to the uneven and rather haphazard system in the Western Shore books before 1768. This and the fact that the debt books appear on the Eastern Shore twenty years ahead of the Western Shore might be attributed to a more efficient, resourceful and methodical Eastern Shore rent-roll keeper. Finally, the existence of Revenue Office copies[63]— duplicate copies—of certain rolls of the Western Shore only may be significant. Possibly it was intended to have copies made of the rent roll books of both shores but only done for the Western Shore books. Perhaps it was not found necessary to copy the Eastern Shore rolls. At any rate, the relatively worse state of Western Shore rent rolls is seen from the following observation in the Minutes of the Board of Revenue for Feb. 23, 1774:

> . . . . . It appearing that the Rentals of the Western Shore was replete with Errors having been kept in a confused State for many years and part of them transcribed by the late Rent Roll Keeper without correcting the same, The Board was informed thereof & order that they be, for the present rectified as often as they shall occur, until a method can be adopted whereby the present Rent Roll Keeper and Farmers of Quit Rents may be enabled to form them on a more regular Plan. . . . .[64]

[63] Cf. Libers 14, 17, 19, 20, 24, 27, 33, 39 and 40 of the *Rent Rolls* series.
[64] *Arch. Md.*, XXXII, 474.

CUSTODIANSHIP

Although the foregoing five series are now and have been for a long time in the custody of the Land Office, such was not always the case. Patents and Warrants have, it is true, always been in the custody of the Land Office. Before the Revolution, Proprietary leases were in the custody of the Secretary or the Agent until, in 1760, the Propretor ordered them deposited in the Land Office.[65] Rent Rolls and Debt Books were successively in the custody of the Secretary, the Agent and the Receiver General. After the Revolution the three latter series presumably fell into the custody of the Western Shore Treasurer who by an Act of 1781 (ch. 20, section 4) was to "have the care and possession of all the debt books and other papers relative to the revenue of the late proprietaries."[66] The Proprietary leases seem after this to have come successively into the custody of the Intendant of the Revenue, the Auditor General and the Clerk of the Council, for in 1829 books and papers of the late Auditor General's office were transferred from the Clerk of the Council to the Register of the Land Office of the Western Shore, the latter being required to take charge of all books and papers which were formerly kept in the Auditor General's office relative to confiscated lands in the state sold by the Intendant of the Revenue or those directly or indirectly connected with the Land Office.[67] Resolution No. 21 for the year 1828 specifically mentions "several Record Books which belonged to the office of the late Auditor General in which are recorded a number of old leases of lands in this state". These, included among the records and papers given over to the Clerk of the Council by the Auditor General's office when it was abolished, are authorized to be delivered by the former to the Register of the Western Shore Land Office. Resolution No. 18 for the year 1832 notes that "there was deposited in the Western Shore Land Office a small number of old leases from the Lord Proprietor of certain individuals for lands lying in the reserves of the State, and whereas the Register of the Land Office was not directed. . . .to record said leases, they. . . .have have never been recorded and as there are many persons deriving their whole title to said lands by said leases it is important that they should be

---

[65] *Ibid.*, IX, 403.

[66] *Kilty*, p. 307.

[67] *Catalogue of Archival Material*, Maryland Hall of Records, 1942, p. 63.

recorded....Resolved....that the Register of the Land Office for the Western Shore be....authorized....to record said leases in a good and sufficient bound book for that purpose...." George G. Brewer was Clerk of the Assembly at this time and, as we have seen, it was he who transcribed the leases as had been authorized. Whether some of the leases were loose papers and some of them already recorded in books as Resolution No. 21 for 1828 seems to indicate, is probably undeterminable, since only Brewer's three-volume transcription appears to be extant.

The date of accession of the *Debt Books* and *Rent Rolls* into the Land Office is not easily ascertained. In 1805 there were two resolutions requiring the Clerk of the Council to examine the debt books and complete the indexes, giving the impression that they were then in his care. Kilty, however, writing in 1808 says, "The register of the land office for the western shore has the care and custody of the records and papers arising under the provincial government, not expressly by any law, passed since the revolution, for that of 1781, gives to the registers the charge only of the short extracts of certificates and grants therein mentioned; but, because the records at large, which have been claimed and kept by the state, naturally fell into the hands of that officer and were indeed, placed in his charge by the governor and council when they were surrendered by the proprietary's officers."[68] In 1819, at any rate, debt books for both shores are acknowledged to be in the Land Office, the Western Shore debt books having just recently been deposited there by the Clerk of the Council.[69] No such exact data can be given as to when and whence the Rent Rolls came to the Land Office. A resolution of 1815 authorized the Register of the Land Office to transcribe certain records including *Anne Arundel County Rent Roll* No. 1, so it is probable all the rent rolls were by then in the custody of the Land Office. One exception to this, of course, is *Rent Roll* Liber O, which was photocopied from Maryland Historical Society originals and added to the *Rent Rolls* series by the present Chief Clerk of the Land Office, Mr. Arthur Trader.

The Land Office itself was housed in the State House at St. Mary's till 1694 when the capital was moved to Annapolis. Then it took up temporary residence in the Anne Arundel County Court-

---

[68] Kilty, pp. 321-2.
[69] *Recorded Laws* Liber T. H. No. 6, pp. 449-50.

house until the new State House was built in 1697. After the State House fire in 1704 the records saved were deposited in the Free School of Annapolis, probably till 1706 when the new capitol was completed.[70] In 1769 a more pretentious State House was built and here the Land Office remained till in 1858 a record office to house the Comptroller's office and the Land Office was authorized.[71] This was situated at the northwest corner of Maryland Avenue and State Circle. When the Court of Appeals building was erected in 1903, the Land Office moved into offices there and remained there till 1935 when it came to its present office in the Hall of Records building.

The records are listed in the following pages in the order in which they appear on the Land Office shelves. The liber number in the margin indicates the present title; the italicized name in the case of the first two series represents the original liber title; in the last three series, Rent Rolls, Debt Books and Proprietary Leases, the italicized name represents the full title as printed on the present binding.

PATENTS SERIES

Liber   0—"Patent Records Original *WC No. 2* 1679 to 1681"; 416 numbered pages; index; title page: "WC No. 2 a Transcribed Record";[72] entries from 1679 to 1681; contains warrants, proofs of rights, assignments, petitions, commissions, letters of Land Office officials.[73]

Liber   1—photocopy of a copy, made in 1724, of missing original Proprietary Records *Liber F* (pp. 1-161) and part of missing original Proprietary Records *Liber B* (pp. 162-640).

Proprietary Records *Liber F*—176 numbered pages according to the original pagination retained in the copy; some 20 scattered pages of the original are not included in the copy, possibly through loss or error

---

[70] *Catalogue of Archival Material*, Maryland Hall of Records, p. 117.

[71] *Ibid.*, p. 87.

[72] This title page is on a sheet of paper completely different from the rest of the book and may represent an error in binding as the book itself has all the earmarks of being an original.

[73] Notation in faded ink at top of pages 84-85 reads: "Mr. Zakaria Cooke of Corke Marchant is Debtor" and "Per Contra is Creditor" suggesting the possibility that this book was originally intended as a merchant's account book.

but more likely due to the copy's being an abridged form of the original;[74] no index; entries from 1636 to 1642; contains proofs of rights, warrants, demands, certificates, patents and assignments as well as commissions, instructions, orders, letters, marriage license applications and other court proceedings, especially in the first and last parts of the book.

Proprietary Records *Liber B*—387 numbered pages, according to the original pagination retained in the copy, followed by some 10 unnumbered pages and these in turn followed by 45 numbered pages at the end of the book containing Acts and Orders of the General Assembly of 1654 and 1657; at p. 48 the page numbering starts over again with 29 but then proceeds regularly;[75] entries from 1646 to 1658; contains demands, proofs of rights, warrants, certificates, caveats, patents, assignments and commissions, but consists mostly of other court proceedings.

Liber 2—photocopy of a copy, made in 1725, of existing original Proprietary Records *Liber Z*[76] (pp. 1-190) and part of existing Proprietary Records *Liber A* (pp. 191-626).

Proprietary Records *Liber Z*—divided into 4 parts: 1) 87 unnumbered pages 2) 59 pages partially numbered, of which 3 are blank and 30 missing, plus an index to the first 45 pages 3) pp. 60-119, with pp. 91 and 119 blank and pp. 92-118 missing 4) pp. 120-130(?) with 8 more missing pages indicated by figures in the index on p. 120;[77] entries from 1637 to 1644; contains all kinds of business of the Province including proclamations, warrants, demands for land and caveats.

Proprietary Records *Liber A*—398 pages, in many cases illegibly numbered, with the first 56 pages miss-

---

[74] Probably by leaving out entries of court proceedings.

[75] About half of these first 48 pages consist of rather regular court proceedings entries from the years 1646 and 1647. Because the rest of the regular entries of Liber B are of 1650 or 1651 and later and because of the early close relationship apparently existing between Libers A and B (as may be noted in the 1680 list) it is possible that some of the missing first 56 pages of Liber A are to be sought here.

[76] The exact title of this book is not known, its present one having been given it by an 18th-century records committee. Since no corresponding volume is mentioned in the 1680 list it may have been lost for a time. The copy in Liber 2 is complete but for the addition of one entry, Sept. 22, 1638 and the exclusion of entries on pp. 9, 32, 79 and pp. 1-3 of Testamentary papers, and the Wills (cf. *Arch. Md.*, I, xiv).

[77] *Arch. Md.*, I, xiv.

ing;[78] fragmentary index; entries from 1647 to 1651; contains demands, patents, commissions, court records, proclamations, assembly proceedings.

Liber   **3**—photocopy of "Liber No. 3 Transcribed from old *Liber A* beginning at fol. 340 to the End and Old *Liber B* from fol. 240 [*sic*] to the End" 1725; 448 pages; this volume represents the completion of the copying of Proprietary Records Liber A begun in Liber 2 and Proprietary Records Liber B begun in Liber 1.

Liber   **4**—photocopy of Liber "A B & H, transcribed from the old record books A, B and H" in 1717; 437 pages; pagination from original books not copied; index; book is divided, by blank spaces or starting of a new page, into 3 parts corresponding to the 3 books copied from: 1) pp. 1-57, containing warrants, demands, certificates, patents and assignments from 1646 to 1650, which constitute an extract of all land business scattered throughout *Liber A* plus one entry at the very beginning which does not appear in *Liber A* and probably comes from one of the missing first 56 pages of that book 2) pp. 57-104, containing entries from 1639 to 1644 of land transactions, which in shortened form are the same entries as those of pp. 28-152 of *Liber F* (not *Liber B* as the title says) 3) pp. 105-436, containing demands, proofs of rights, warrants, certificates, patents and assignments from the years 1650 to 1655; presumably a copy of original *Liber H* which according to the 1680 list covered the years 1650 to 1655.[79] The last page of this volume contains "an Abstract of the Certificates that were in the Land Record Liber L", "an old thin Parchment Covered Book", most of them being from the year 1657 or a few years earlier thus corresponding to the *Liber L* of the 1680 list.

Liber   **5**—photocopy of a copy transcribed probably in 1717[80] from original *Liber Q*;[81] 480 numbered pages; pagination of original not kept; index; entries for 1658; contains

---

[78] In the original 58 pages are missing, but. 57-8 are to be found in the Liber 2 copy.

[79] Apparently some pages are missing. The first entry is referred to in *Rent Rolls 0*, p. 108 as being on p. 3 of "Record for land for 1650" (Liber H).

[80] The inscription on the flyleaf "This book is Transcribed from the Old Record Book Liber Q" is in the same hand as the parallel inscription in Liber 4, done in 1717.

[81] The original is extant but almost half missing, beginning with what is p. 215 of the copy.

patents, certificates, warrants, assignments, demands, commissions and instructions from Lord Baltimore.

Liber   **6**—photocopy of a copy, made in 1725, of existing original *Liber R*[82] (pp. 1-540) and part of existing original *Liber X* (pp. 541-627). *Liber R*—211 numbered double pages; first 4 pages missing in original but the 4th missing page is supplied in the copy; index in original but not in copy; entries from 1659; contains demands, warrants, certificates, patents, assignments.

          Liber X—429 pages with an apparently definite end of the book at p. 429 but with index references to pp. 433, 434, 435 as well[83]; index in original but not in copy; entries from 1661 to 1663; contains demands, warrants, certificates, patents, assignments. The original of *Liber X* constitutes Liber 1 of the *Warrants* Series.

Liber   **7**—photocopy of a copy, made in 1725, of parts of existing original *Liber X* (pp. 1-343) and existing original *Liber AA* (pp. 344-639).

          Liber X—cf. under Liber 6 above.

          Liber AA—532 numbered pages; index in original but not in copy; entries from 1633 to 1664; contains demands, warrants, proofs of rights, certificates, patents, assignments, caveats.

Liber   **8**—photocopy of a copy, made in 1726, of pp. 302-532 of existing original *Liber AA*; 347 pages; cf. under Liber 7 above.

Liber   **9**—photocopy of a copy, made in 1725, of pp. 1-720 of existing original *Liber CC;* 640 pages; entries from 1664 to 1665; index in original but not in copy; contains demands, warrants, proofs of rights, certificates, patents and assignments.

Liber   **10**—photocopy of a copy, made in 1726, of pp. 1-519 of existing original *Liber DD* and pp. 720-828 of existing original *Liber CC;* 518 pages.

          Liber DD—519 pages; entries from 1665; index in original but not in copy; contains demands, warrants,

---

[82] The present binding labels this volume as Liber RX, probably due to the influence of having both R and X copied together in Liber 6. The 1680 list of course mentions no Liber RX, simply Liber R 1659.

[83] The entries are in a hand different from that of the normal index entries, indicating that they were added later with the intention of adding the corresponding entries later or with the aim of identifying some loose leaves inserted between the last pages of the book.

proofs of rights, certificates, patents, assignments. *Liber CC*—cf. under Liber 9 above.

Liber 11—photocopy of a copy, made in 1726, of existing original *Liber EE* (518 pages) ; 516 pages; entries from 1665 to 1666; index in original but not in copy; contains warrants, certificates, proofs of rights, patents, assignments, caveats, instructions from Lord Baltimore.

Liber 12—photocopy of a copy, made in 1725, of existing original *Liber FF* and part of existing original *Liber GG;* 638 pages.

Liber FF—572 pages; entries from 1666 to 1667; index in original but not in copy; contains demands, proofs of rights, certificates, warrants, patents, assignments. *Liber GG*—pp. 1-70; cf. description under Liber 13 below.

Liber 13—photocopy of a copy, made in 1725, of pp. 70-549 of existing original *Liber GG;* 586 pages.

Liber GG—549 pages; entries from 1667 to 1669; index in original but not in copy; contains demands, warrants, proofs of rights, certificates, patents, assignments.

Liber 14—photocopy of a copy, made in 1725, of pp. 1-508 of existing original *Liber HH* and pp. 1-315 of existing original *Liber JJ;* 638 pages.

Liber HH—508 pages; entries from 1668 to 1670; no index; contains proofs of rights, warrants, certificates, patents, assignments, depositions, indentures. *Liber JJ*—540 pages; entries from 1670 to 1671; index in original but not in copy; contains proofs of rights, warrants, certificates, patents, assignments, petitions.

Liber 15—photocopy of a copy, made in 1726, of pp. 315-540 of existing original *Liber JJ;* 133 pages.
Liber JJ—cf. under Liber 14 above.

Liber 16—photocopy of a copy, made in 1726, of existing original *Liber KK;* 551 pages.

Liber KK—501 pages; entries from 1670 to 1672; contains a few examples of all the usual types of land business but mostly patents; index in original but not in copy.

Liber 18—transcript, known as B No. 15, Part I, made in 1836, of part of a copy, made in 1726 and known as Liber

No. 15 or Liber A No. 15, of pp. 1-458 of existing original *Liber LL;* 464 pages.

Liber LL—913 pages; entries from 1673 to 1678; complete index in original, none in 1726 copy and index to certificates and patents only in 1836 copy; contains all the usual types of land entries but mostly patents and certificates.

Liber 18a—transcript, known as Liber No. 15, Part II, made in 1836, of remainder of copy, 1726, of remaining pp. 458-913 of existing original *Liber LL;* pp. 465-909; cf. Liber 18 above.

Liber 19—photocopy of a copy, made in 1726, of pp. 1-673 of existing original *Liber WT;* 640 pages.

Liber WT—901 pages; entries from 1670 to 1673; index in original but not in copy; contains proofs of rights, warrants, certificates, patents, assignments.

Liber 20—photocopy of a copy, made about 1726, of pp. 674-901 of existing original *Liber WT* and pp. 1-536 of existing original *Liber MM;* 638 pages.

Liber WT—cf. under Liber 19 above.

Liber MM—893 pages; entries from 1672 to 1675; no index; contains proofs of rights, warrants, certificates, patents, assignments.

Liber 21—photocopy of a copy, made in 1726, of pp. 537-893 of existing original *Liber MM;* 387 pages; cf. under Liber 20 above.

Liber 22—photocopy of a copy, made in 1726, of pp. 1-500 of existing original *Liber WC;* 638 pages.

Liber WC—899 pages according to original pagination noted in the copy, of which some 16 are missing in the original but preserved in the copy; entries from 1675 to 1680; contains proofs of rights, warrants, certificates, patents, assignments, a few indentures and a great number of resurvey warrants.

Liber 23—photocopy of a copy, made in 1727, of pp. 500-899 of existing original *Liber WC;* 412 pages; cf. under Liber 22 above.

Liber 24—photocopy of a copy, made in 1726, of existing originals *Liber WC No. 3* and *Liber WC No. 5;* 555 pages.

Liber WC No. 3—515 pages; entries from 1679 to 1680; index in original but not in copy; contains patents and certificates and related assignments.

Liber WC No. 5—516 pages; entries from 1679 to 1683; index in original but not in copy; contains certificates and some assignments.

Liber 25—photocopy of a copy, made in 1726, of existing originals *Liber SD No. A and Liber DS No. B;* 445 pages.

Liber SD No. A—509 pages; entries from 1682 to 1685; 2 indexes in original but none in copy; contains certificates and related assignments.

Liber DS No.B—537 pages; entries from 1685 to 1688; index in original but not in copy; contains certificates and related assignments.

Liber 26—photocopy of a copy, made in 1726 and known as Liber A No. 23, of existing original *Liber B No. 2;* 281 pages.

Liber B No. 2—337 pages; entries from 1694 to 1695; index in original but not in copy; contains patents from 1694-5 and related assignments and certificates of earlier date and 2 special grants of 1693.

Liber 27—transcribed copy, made in 1835 and known as Liber No. 23 B, of Liber A No. 23, the 1726 copy of *Liber B No. 2;* cf. Liber 26 above.

Liber 28—*Liber CB No. 2;* 544 pages; index; entries from 1680 to 1681; contains patents.

Liber 29—*Liber CB No. 3;* 528 pages; index; entries from 1681 to 1684; contains patents.

Liber 30—*Liber IB & IL No. C;* 404 pages; index; entries from 1684 to 1700, plus one patent on flyleaf dated 1705; contains patents.

Liber 31—*Liber SD No. A;* 539 pages; index; entries from 1683 to 1684; contains patents.

Liber 32—*Liber NS No. B;* 717 pages; index; entries from 1684 to 1689; contains patents.

Liber 33—*Liber NS No. 2;* 738 pages; index; entries from 1685 to 1688; contains patents.

Liber 34—*Liber WD;* 535 pages; index; entries from 1689 to 1706; contains patents and a few indentures.

Liber 35—*Liber DS No. F;* 543 pages, plus 2 pages written upside down at end of book and a title page which appears to read "Liber CL No. 1"; index; contains warrants and assignments from 1685 to 1689 and, separated by 2 blank pages, patents from 1702 to 1704.

Liber **37**—*Liber BB No. 3-B;* 548 pages; index; entries from 1694 to 1699; contains patents and their related certificates and assignments.

Liber **38**—*Liber CC No. 4;* 163 pages; index; entries from 1695 to 1700; contains patents, indentures, certificates and assignments and some instructions from Lord Baltimore.

Liber **39**—photocopy of a copy, made in 1727, of existing original *Liber CD No. 4;* 319 pages.
Liber CD No. 4; 545 pages; index in original but not in copy; entries from 1695 to 1707; blank space for pp. 79-80 because "in the Original Record Book the leafe is there Cutt out"; contains patents and related certificates and assignments.

Liber **40**—copy, made in 1770, of existing original *Liber C No. 3;* 603 pages.
Liber C No. 3—646 pages; index in both original and copy; entries from 1695 to 1696; contains patents with related certificates and assignments.

Liber **41, Part I**—*Liber DD No. 5;* pp. 1-458; entries from 1700 to 1707 according to date of issue of patents; contains certificates and assignments and date of patents' issue.

Liber 41½, Part II—*Liber DD No. 5;* pp. 459-845; entries from 1707 to 1713 as in Liber 41; index to complete volume.

Liber **42**—*Liber EE No. 6;* 334 pages; index; entries from 1713 to 1716 according to date of issue of patents; contains certificates and assignments and date of patents' issue.

Liber **43**—*Liber FF No. 7;* 433 pages; index; entries from 1716 to 1722 according to date of issue of patents; contains certificates and assignments and date of patents' issue.

Liber **44**—*Liber PL No. 2;* 347 pages; index; entries from 1706 to 1708; contains patents.

Liber **45**—photocopy of existing original *Liber PL No. 3;* 539 pages; index; entries from 1708 to 1714; contains patents.

Liber **46**—*Liber PL No. 4;* 446 pages; index; one entry, 1710; all other entries from 1715 to 1721; contains patents.

Liber **47**—*Liber PL No. 5;* 853 pages; index; entries from 1722 to 1726; contains patents.

Liber   **48**—photocopy of *Liber PL No. 6;* 644 pages; entries from 1724 to 1728; index; contains patents.

Liber   **49**—*Liber PL No. 7;* 640 pages; index; entries from 1727 to 1730; contains patents.

Liber   **50**—*Liber PL No. 8;* 836 pages; index; entries from 1730 to 1734; patents.

Liber   **51**—*Liber RY No. 1;* 543 pages; index; entries from 1710 to 1718; patents.

Liber   **52**—*Liber CE No. 1;* 433 pages; index; entries from 1714 to 1722; patents.

Liber   **53**—*Liber IL No. A;* 870 pages; index; entries from 1716 to 1728; certificates and assignments.

Liber   **54**—*Liber IL No. B;* 508 pages; index; entries from 1723 to 1731; certificates and assignments.

Liber   **55**—*Liber AM No. 1;* 410 pages; index; entries from 1726 to 1735; certificates and assignments.

Liber   **56**—*Liber EI No. 1;* 534 pages; index; entries from 1732 to 1734; patents; 4 pages of a hearing on a land dispute, April 1722, added at end of book.

Liber   **57**—*Liber EI No. 2;* 929 pages; index; entries from 1734 to 1739; patents.

Liber   **58**—*Liber EI No. 3;* 539 pages; index; entries from 1730 to 1737; certificates and assignments.

Liber   **59**—*Liber EI No. 4;* 542 pages; 2 indexes; entries from 1734 to 1740; patents.

Liber   **60**—*Liber EI No. 5;* 580 pages; index; entries from 1734 to 1741; certificates and assignments.

Liber   **61**—photocopy of *Liber EI No. 6;* 732 pages; entries from 1737 to 1744; patents; no index.

Liber   **62**—*Liber LG No. B;* 779 pages; no index; entries from 1739 to 1744; patents.

Liber   **63**—*Liber LG No. C;* 717 pages; index; entries from 1739 to 1747; certificates and assignments; patents on pp. 464-599.

Liber   **64**—*Liber LG No. E;* 748 pages; index; entries from 1741 to 1746; certificates and assignments.

Liber   **65**—copy, made in 1814, of *Liber PT No. 1;* 352 pages in both original and copy; index; entries from 1743 to 1747; patents.

Liber **66**—*Liber PT No. 2;* 339 pages; index; entries from 1742 to 1746; patents.

Liber **67**—*Liber BT & BY No. 3;* 732 pages; index; entries from 1745 to 1748; patents.

Liber **68**—*Liber TI No. 1;* 538 pages; 2 indexes; entries from 1743 to 1748; certificates and assignments; patents from pp. 57-114.

Liber **69**—*Liber TI No. 3;* 532 pages; index; entries from 1746 to 1749; patents.

Liber **70**—*Liber TI No. 4;* 743 pages; index; entries from 1746 to 1752; patents.

Liber **71**—photocopy of a copy of *Liber BY & GS No. 1;* 686 pages; no index; entries from 1746 to 1750; certificates and assignments.

Liber **72**—*Liber BY & GS No. 2;* 737 pages; index; entries from 1747 to 1751; patents.

Liber **73**—*Liber BY & GS No. 3;* 731 pages; index; entries from 1748 to 1762; patents.

Liber **74**—*Liber BY & GS No. 4;* 707 pages; index; entries from 1748 to 1754; patents.

Liber **75**—photocopy of a copy of *Liber BY & GS No. 5;* 656 pages; no index; entries from 1748 to 1752; certificates and assignments.

Liber **76**—*Liber Y & S No. 6;* 532 pages; no index; entries from 1752 to 1755; patents.

Liber **77**—*Liber Y & S No. 7;* 513 pages; index; entries from 1751 to 1753; certificates and assignments.

Liber **78**—*Liber Y & S No. 8;* 723 pages; index; entries from 1752 to 1754; patents.

Liber **79**—*Liber GS No. 1;* 435 pages; index; entries from 1748 to 1753; certificates and assignments.

Liber **80**—*Liber GS No. 2;* 446 pages; index; entries from 1753 to 1755; patents.

Liber **81**—*Liber BC & GS No. 1;* 428 pages; index; entries from 1751 to 1756; certificates and assignments.

Liber **82**—*Liber BC & GS No. 2;* 515 pages; index; entries from 1753 to 1756; patents.

Liber   **83**—*Liber BC & GS No. 3;* 354 pages; index; entries from 1753 to 1760; patents.

Liber   **84**—*Liber BC & GS No. 4;* 344 pages; index; entries from 1753 to 1755; certificates and assignments.

Liber   **85**—*Liber BC & GS No. 5;* 332 pages; index; entries from 1754 to 1757; certificates and assignments.

Liber   **86**—*Liber BC & GS No. 6;* 525 pages; index; entries from 1753 to 1757; patents.

Liber   **87**—*Liber BC & GS No. 7;* 532 pages; no index; entries from 1753 to 1760; patents.

Liber   **88**—*Liber BC & GS No. 8;* 738 pages; index; entries from 1755 to 1763; patents.

Liber   **89**—*Liber BC & GS No. 9;* 546 pages; index; entries from 1754 to 1758; certificates and assignments.

Liber   **90**—*Liber BC & GS No. 10;* 746 pages; index; entries from 1756 to 1763; patents.

Liber   **91**—*Liber BC & GS No. 11;* 342 pages; index; entries from 1758 to 1759; certificates and assignments.

Liber   **92**—*Liber BC & GS No. 12;* 544 pages; index; entries from 1759 to 1760; certificates and assignments.

Liber   **93**—*Liber BC & GS No. 13;* 753 pages; index; entries from 1758 to 1762; patents.

Liber   **94**—*Liber BC & GS No. 14;* 716 pages; index; entries from 1761 to 1762; certificates and assignments.

Liber   **95**—*Liber BC & GS No. 15;* 819 pages; index; entries from 1759 to 1763; patents; exchange of letters with Governor Sharpe concerning a land dispute on the last pages.

Liber   **96**—*Liber BC & GS No. 16;* 732 pages; index; entries from 1759 to 1768; patents.

Liber   **97**—*Liber BC & GS No. 17;* 734 pages; index; entries from 1759 to 1763; patents.

Liber   **98**—*Liber BC & GS No. 18;* 720 pages; index; entries from 1761 to 1764; patents.

Liber   **99**—*Liber BC & GS No. 19;* 700 pages; index; entries from 1761 to 1764; certificates and assignments.

Liber 100—*Liber BC & GS No. 20;* 722 pages; index; entries from 1761 to 1765; patents.

Liber 101—*Liber BC & GS No. 21;* 717 pages; index; entries from 1761 to 1763; certificates and assignments.

Liber 102—photocopy of *Liber BC & GS No. 22;* 712 pages; index; entries from 1761 to 1767; patents.

Liber 103—*Liber BC & GS No. 23;* 715 pages; index; entries from 1762 to 1765; patents.

Liber 104—*Liber BC & GS No. 24;* 707 pages; index; entries from 1762 to 1765; certificates and assignments.

Liber 105—*Liber BC & GS No. 25;* 495 pages; entries from 1763 to 1765; index; patents.

Liber 106—photocopy of *Liber BC & GS No. 26;* 520 pages; no index; entries from 1762 to 1767; patents.

Liber 107—*Liber BC & GS No. 27;* 617 pages; index; entries from 1762 to 1765; certificates and assignments.

Liber 108—*Liber BC & GS No. 28;* 612 pages; index; entries from 1760 to 1767; patents.

Liber 109—*Liber BC & GS No. 29;* 519 pages; index; entries from 1764 to 1768; patents.

Liber 110—*Liber BC & GS No. 30;* 497 pages; index; entries from 1764 to 1766; certificates and assignments.

Liber 111—*Liber BC & GS No. 31;* 498 pages; index; entries from 1765 to 1768; patents.

Liber 112—*Liber BC & GS No. 32;* 552 pages; index; entries from 1765 to 1768; patents.

Liber 113—*Liber BC & GS No. 33;* 526 pages; index; entries from 1765 to 1769; patents.

Liber 114—*Liber BC & GS No. 34;* 492 pages; index; entries from 1765 to 1768; certificates and assignments.

Liber 115—*Liber BC & GS No. 35;* 548 pages; index; entries from 1767 to 1770; patents.

Liber 116—*Liber BC & GS No. 36;* 503 pages; index; entries from 1768 to 1770; patents.

Liber 117—*Liber BC & GS No. 37;* 507 pages; index; entries from 1768 to 1769; certificates and assignments.

Liber 118—*Liber BC & GS No. 38;* 522 pages; index; entries from 1768 to 1771; patents.

Liber 119—*Liber BC & GS No. 39;* 529 pages; index; entries from 1769 to 1772; patents.

Liber 120—*Liber BC & GS No. 40;* 502 pages; index; entries from 1768 to 1771; certificates and assignments.

Liber 121—*Liber BC & GS No. 41;* 501 pages; index; entries from 1769 to 1771; certificates and assignments.

Liber 122—*Liber BC & GS. No. 42;* 518 pages; index; entries from 1770 to 1773; patents; last page missing.

Liber 123—*Liber BC & GS No. 43;* 535 pages; index; entries from 1770 to 1773; patents.

Liber 124—*Liber BC & GS No. 44;* 538 pages; index; entries from 1772 to 1774; patents.

Liber 125—*Liber BC & GS No. 45;* 500 pages; index; entries from 1171 to 1774; certificates and assignments.

Liber 126—*Liber BC & GS No. 46;* 527 pages; index; entries from 1773 to 1774; patents.

Liber 127—*Liber BC & GS No. 47;* 519 pages; index; entries from 1771 to 1774; certificates and assignments.

Liber 128—*Liber BC & GS No. 48;* 528 pages; index; entries from 1770 to 1775; patents.

Liber 129—*Liber BC & GS No. 49;* 565 pages; index; entries from 1770 to 1777; patents.

Liber 130—*Liber BC & GS No. 50;* 486 pages; index; entries from 1772 to 1782; certificates and assignments.

Liber 131—*Liber BC & GS No. 51;* 510 pages; index; entries from 1773 to 1777; certificates and assignments.

Liber 132—*Liber BC & GS No. 52;* 514 pages; index; entries from 1775 to 1777; patents; letter at end of book requesting Benedict Calvert to turn over the Land Office records to the new Register, Mr. Saint George Peale.

WARRANTS SERIES

Liber   1—*Liber X* "Record for Land 1661-1663"; 429 numbered pages; index; entries from 1661 to 1663; contains entry rights, warrants, certificates, patents, assignments, letters and orders from Lord Baltimore.[84]

Liber   2—photocopy of a copy, made in 1726, of existing original *Liber WC No. 2;*[85] index not included in the copy.

---

[84] Cf. Libers 6 and 7 of the *Patents* series.
[85] Cf. Liber 0 of the *Patents* series.

Liber 3—*Liber CB* 1679-1683; 321 numbered pages; index; entries from 1679 to 1683; contains petitions, mandamus orders, proceedings of the Land Council and resurveys; on flyleaf is list of books turned over to the Register of the Land Office in 1680.

Liber 4—*Liber CB* 1683-1684; 383 numbered pages; index; contains entries from 1683 to 1684; petitions, mandamus orders, proceedings of the Land Council and resurveys.

Liber 5—*Liber WC No. 4;* 521 numbered pages; index; entries from 1681 to 1685; contains warrants, assignments, a few caveats and deputy surveyors' bonds.

Liber 6—*Liber A;* 493 numbered pages; index; entries from 1694 to 1706; contains various kinds of warrants and related assignments.

Liber 7—*Liber AA;* 440 pages; index; entries from 1706 to 1715; contains various kinds of warrants, especially resurveys and warrant renewments, and related assignments.

Liber 8—photocopy of a copy, made in 1727, of existing original *Liber BB.*
Liber *BB*—357 pages; entries from 1715 to 1722; no index; contains various kinds of warrants and their related assignments, plus 2 letters from Lord Baltimore to Charles Carroll.

Liber 9—*Liber CC;* 423 pages; index; entries from 1722 to 1725; contains warrants, instructions from Lord Baltimore and a few petitions and commissions. 88 pages of numbered warrants roughly bound forming a separate booklet, are to be found in the front of this book. They appear to be the rough draft of warrants, dated 1798-1800, "recorded in Eastern Shore Warrants 8 beginning f.34" as a notation on the flyleaf correctly says.

Liber 10—*Liber DD;* 420 pages; index; entries from 1725 to 1729; contains warrants, especially resurveys and renewments, and some instructions and commissions.

Liber 11—*Liber EE;* 526 pages; index; entries from 1729 to 1735; contains warrants as above, and some commissions and instructions.

Liber 12—*Liber FF;* 354 pages, pp. 63-86 bound in upside down and in reverse order; entries from 1735 to 1738; index; contains warrants and a few commissions.

Liber   **13**—*Liber LG A;* 364 pages; no index; contains entries from 1738 to 1742; warrants and a few instructions and commissions.

Liber   **14**—*Liber LG No. D;* 530 pages; index; entries from 1742 to 1745; contains warrants, a few instructions and commissions and related Chancery Court proceedings.

Liber   **15**—photocopy of *Liber PT 3;* 660 pages; entries from 1745 to 1748; no index; contains warrants and a few letters and instructions from Lord Baltimore and some related Chancery Court proceedings.

Liber   **16**—*Liber TI 2;* 688 pages; index; entries from 1748 to 1751; contains warrants and a few instructions and commissions.

Liber   **17**—*Liber TI 5;* 524 pages; no index; entries from 1751 to 1752; contents as in Liber 16 above.

Liber   **18**—*Liber TI 6;* 539 pages; index; entries from 1752 to 1754; contents as above.

Liber   **19**—*Liber TI 7;* 347 pages; index; entries from 1754 to 1755; contents as above.

Liber   **20**—*Liber TI 8;* 259 pages; no index; entries from 1755 to 1756; contents as above.

Liber   **21**—photocopy of *Liber TI 9;* 263 pages; no index; entries from 1756 to 1757; contents as above.

Liber   **22**—*Liber TI 10;* 160 pages; index; entries for 1757; contents as above.

Liber   **23**—*Liber TI 11;* 440 pages; index; entries from 1757 to 1758; contents as above.

Liber   **24**—*Liber TI 12;* 515 pages; index; entries for 1759; contents as above.

Liber   **25**—*Liber WS 1;* 516 pages; no index; entries for 1760; contents as above.

Liber   **26**—*Liber WS 2;* 343 pages; index; entries from 1761 to 1762; contents as above.

Liber   **27**—*Liber WS 3;* 349 pages; index; entries for 1761; contents as above.

Liber   **28**—*Liber WS 4;* 526 pages; index; entries from 1761 to 1762; contents as above.

Liber   **29**—*Liber WS 5;* 346 pages; no index; entries from 1762 to 1763; contents as above.

Liber **30**—*Liber WS 6;* 816 pages; index; entries from 1763 to 1764; contents as above.

Liber **31**—*Liber WS 7;* 534 pages; no index; entries from 1764 to 1765; contents as above.

Liber **32**—*Liber WS 8;* 488 pages; index; entries from 1765 to 1766; contents as above.

Liber **33**—*Liber WS 9;* 596 pages; index; entries from 1766 to 1767; contents as above.

Liber **34**—*Liber WS 10;* 384 pages; index; entries from 1767; contents as above.

Liber **35**—*Liber WS 11;* 311 pages; index; entries from 1768; contents as above.

Liber **36**—*Liber WS 12;* 301 pages; index; entries from 1768 to 1769; contents as above.

Liber **37**—*Liber WS 13;* 400 pages; index; entries from 1769 to 1770; contents as above.

Liber **38**—*Liber WS 14;* 316 pages; index; entries from 1770; contents as above.

Liber **39**—*Liber WS 15;* 301 pages; index; entries from 1770 to 1771; contents as above.

Liber **40**—*Liber WS 16;* 425 pages; index; entries from 1771 to 1773; contents as above.

Liber **41**—*Liber WS 17;* 342 pages; index; entries from 1773 to 1774; contents as above.

Liber **42**—*Liber DS 1;* 290 pages; index; entries from 1775; contents as above.

PROPRIETARY LEASES SERIES (1707-1777)

1—*Proprietary Leases Liber GGB A;* 721 pages; typed index of tract names; contains leases from Baltimore County of lessees A through K.

2—*Proprietary Leases Liber GGB B;* 777 pages; typed index of tract names; contains leases from Baltimore County of lessees L through Y.

3—*Proprietary Leases Liber GGB C;* 646 pages; typed index of tract names, plus handwritten index of lessees' names; contains leases from Cecil, Anne Arundel, Kent, Queen Anne's, Dorchester, Charles, St. Mary's, Somerset, Worcester and Prince George's counties.

RENT ROLL SERIES

Liber   **0**—*Rent Roll St. Mary's, Charles, Calvert Counties and Isle of Kent.*
Photocopy of four small original books bound into one volume of 115 re-numbered pages; typed index of tract names and owners of land.

     (1) St. Mary's County Rent Roll.   35 originally numbered pages; contains a record of the rent due on each piece of land in the county, including a short history of the land: proof of rights, certificates of survey, patents and alienations; entries are of land patented between 1639 and 1659.

     (2) Charles County Rent Roll. 27 originally numbered pages; contains same material as (1) above; entries are of land patented between 1642 and 1659.

     (3) Calvert County Rent Roll. 41 originally numbered pages, pp. 9 and 37 blank, four p. 24's; contains same material as above; entries are of land patented between 1642 and 1658.

     (4) Isle of Kent Rent Roll. ' 11 originally numbered pages; contains same material as above; entries are of land patented between 1640 and 1658.

Liber   **1**—*Rent Roll Anne Arundel Baltimore No. 1.* 283 numbered pages; typed index of tract names.

     (1) Anne Arundel County Rent Roll.   Pages 1-190; contains entries of lands patented between 1651 and 1746; alienations to 1774.

     (2) Baltimore County Rent Roll.   Pages 191-283; contains entries on lands patented between 1658 and 1746; alienations to 1773.

Liber   **2**—*Rent Roll Vol. 2 Anne Arundel Baltimore No. 2.* **Pages** 285-560, being the completion of preceding Liber 1; typed index of tract names; contains earlier supplementary entries from Baltimore County; alienations to 1771. Re-numbering of pages of this and the preceding volume, various referrings-back and reverse chronological order of entries indicate a change from a former binding arrangement (both in one volume).

Liber   **3**—*Rent Roll Vol. 1 Calvert, Prince George, Frederick No. 1.* 282 pages, pp. 99, 115-121, 148-203 blank; typed index of tract names. Re-numbering of pages of this volume and the following volume, various referrings-back and reverse chronological order of entries indicate Libers 3 and 4 were formerly bound together in one volume.

    (1) Calvert County Rent Roll. Pages 1-98; contains entries on lands patented between 1651 and 1751; alienations to 1776.

    (2) Frederick County Rent Roll. Pages 122-147; contains entries on lands patented 1748-1751; no alienations.

    (3) Prince George's County Rent Roll. Pages 100-114, 205-282; contains entries on lands patented 1742-1751; alienations to 1750.

Liber 4—*Rent Roll Vol. 2 Calvert, Prince George, Frederick No. 2.* Pages 283-566, being the completion of preceding Liber 3; contains entries on lands from Prince George's County only, patented 1651 to 1749; a few alienations to 1772; typed index of tract names.

Liber 5—*Rent Roll Vol. 1 Kent, Cecil No. 1.* Pages 1-206; contains (pp. 1-204) entries on lands in Kent County patented between 1658 and 1775, including some forty "Additional Rent Rolls" submitted between 1734 and 1776 and (pp. 205-206) the names, owners and acreages of lands patented between 1782 and 1790; typed index of tract names. Pagination of this and the following volume (Liber 6) indicates the two were once bound together as one volume.

Liber 6—*Rent Roll Vol. 2 Kent, Cecil No. 2.* Pages 288-471; typed index of tract names; contains (pp. 295-460) entries on lands in Cecil County patented between 1658-1775, including some forty "Additional Rent Rolls" submitted annually between 1734 and 1776 and (pp. 461-471) the names, owners and acreages of lands patented between 1782-1790. On pp. 348-354 is the rent roll of Durham County, Delaware.

Liber 7 & 8—*Rent Roll Vol. 1 & 2 St. Mary's Charles No. 1 & 2.* Typed index of tract names.

    (1) St. Mary's Rent Roll. Pages 1-118; entries on lands patented between 1639 and 1751; alienations to 1771.

    (2) Charles County Rent Roll. Pages 283-464; entries on lands patented between 1642 and 1751; alienations to 1775.

Liber 9—*Rent Roll Vol. 1 Somerset Dorchester No. 1.* 272 pages; typed index of tract names; entries on lands in Somerset County patented between 1662 and 1721; alienations to 1772.

Liber 10—*Rent Roll Vol. 2 Somerset Dorchester No. 2.* Pages 273-569; typed index of tract names. Pagination indicates this and Liber 9 were one volume.

    (1) Somerset Rent Roll. Pages 273-342 (pp. 330-335 are remarked as being copied here by mistake instead of in the Additional Rent Roll—Liber 45); entries on lands patented up to 1730; alienations to 1772.

    (2) Dorchester Rent Roll. Pages 343-569 (pp. 566-9 are remarked as being copied here by mistake instead of in the Additional Rent Roll—Liber 29); entries on lands patented between 1659 and 1730; alienations to 1772.

Liber 11—*Rent Roll Vol. 1 Talbot Queen Anne No.1.* Pages 4-287; entries on lands in Talbot County patented up to 1775, including Additional Rent Rolls from 1734 to 1775; pp. 285-7 has the names, acreages and owners of lands patented 1782-1790; typed index of tract names. Pagination and title of this volume indicate that it and the following Liber 12 were once bound together in one volume.

Liber 12—*Rent Roll Vol. 2 Talbot Queen Anne No.2.* Pages 297-562; entries on lands in Queen Anne's County patented up to 1750, including Additional Rent Rolls from 1734-1750; alienations to 1772; typed index of tract names.[86]

Liber 12A—*Talbot and Queen Anne Counties Rent Roll No. 3.* 165 pages; typed index of tract names; entries on lands patented in Queen Anne's County up to 1755. This volume and Libers 25 and 37 are unique in this series in having entries arranged alphabetically according to the name of the person paying the rent. No alienations.

Liber 13—*Rent Roll Anne Arundel No. 3.* 132 pages; typed index of tract names; title page: "Anne Arundel County Rent Roll Lib. No. 2 Anno 1756;" entries on lands patented from 1753 to 1768 (pp. 1-69), additional annual rent rolls from 1769 to 1775 (pp. 70-124) and names, owners and acreages of tracts patented between 1782 and 1790. Alienations to 1776.

---

[86] The Hall of Records has among its miscellaneous records a partially copied rent roll for Queen Anne's County which may have been intended as a Revenue Office copy of Liber 12 or 12A.

Liber **14**—*Rent Roll Anne Arundel No. 4.* 228 pages; typed index of tract names; title page: "Anne Arundel County Rent Roll 1753;" entries on lands patented up to 1755 plus half a dozen from 1766-7; alienations to 1768. This is the Revenue Office counterpart of Liber 16.

Liber **15**—*Rent Roll Anne Arundel No. 5.* 223 pages; typed index of tract names; contains rent roll entries on lands patented up to 1743; alienations to 1737.

Liber **16**—*Rent Roll Anne Arundel No. 6.* 233 pages; typed index of tract names; title page: "Anne Arundel County rent roll to Michaelmass, 1753;" contains rent roll entries on land patented up to 1755 plus half a dozen from 1766-7; alienations to 1774; pp. 228-233 additional alienations, a computation of the total amount of the rent roll and memoranda concerning various tracts not in the debt books or lying in other counties, etc.

Liber **17**—*Rent Roll Anne Arundel No. 7.* 69 pages; typed index of tract names; title page: "Anne Arundel County Rent Roll Vol. 2d. 1756;" contains entries on lands patented 1753-1768; alienations to 1768. This book is the Revenue Office counterpart of Liber 13, pp. 1-69.

Liber **18**—*Rent Roll Baltimore No. 1.* 417 pages; typed index of tract names; title page: "Baltimore County Rent Roll to Michaelmass 1753;" entries on lands patented up to 1759; alienations to 1774.

Liber **19**—*Rent Roll Baltimore No. 2.* Pages 301-613; typed index of tract names; entries on lands patented up to 1771; alienations to 1770. This is the Revenue Office counterpart of pp. 1-187 of Liber 21 and is the continuation of Liber 20.

Liber **20**—*Rent Roll Baltimore No. 3.* 300 pages; typed index of tract names; title page: "Baltimore County Rent Roll 1753;" alienations to 1770; entries on lands patented up to 1759. This is the Revenue Office counterpart of Liber 18, pp. 1-300.

Liber **21**—*Rent Roll Baltimore No. 4.* 243 pages; typed index of tract names; contains entries on lands patented up to 1768 plus additional rent rolls for 1769-1773, plus one entry for 1783; alienations to 1774. This is the continuation of Liber 18.

Liber **22**—*Rent Roll Baltimore No. 5.* 66 pages; typed index of tract names; contains the Additional Rent Rolls of 1774 and 1775 plus entries of names, owners and acreages of lands patented between 1782 and 1790.

Liber   **23**—*Rent Roll Calvert No. 3.* 2 rent rolls with typed index of tract names of both.

     (1) pp. 1-85; entries on lands patented up to 1751; list of names and tracts not on rent roll; no alienations.

     (2) pp. 180; title page: "Calvert County Rent Roll to Michaelmass Anno 1753;" entries on lands patented up to 1765; names and tracts not on rent roll; alienations up to 1776; computation of total rent roll.

Liber   **24**—*Rent Roll Calvert No. 4.* 80 pages; typed index of tract names; title page: "Calvert County Rent Roll Anno 1753;" rent roll entries on lands patented up to 1768 plus names, owners and acreages of lands patented between 1784 and 1788; alienations to 1768. Pages 1-78 are the Revenue Office counterpart of pages 1-78 of the second part of Liber 23.

Liber   **25**—*Rent Roll Cecil No. 4.* Typed index of tract names. This volume is in two parts:

     (1) Pages 1-64; entries on lands patented up to 1759 in Cecil County; no alienations. Arrangement is alphabetical by name of person paying rent on the land, but the names of the persons are not entered beyond the first two letters of the alphabet.

     (2) Pages 101-203 (pp. 65-100 are blank); entries on lands patented up to 1756 in Kent County. Arrangement is apparently meant to have been alphabetical by name of person paying rent as in the first part of the volume but no names or alienations are entered.

Liber   **26**—*Rent Roll Charles No. 1.* 194 pages; typed index of tract names; title page: "The Rent Roll of Charles County to Michaelmass Anno Domini 1753;" rent roll entries on lands patented to 1753 (pp. 1-161), additional rent rolls from 1753 to 1766 and the computation of the 1753 rent roll; alienations to 1775.

Liber   **27**—*Rent Roll Charles No. 2.* 205 pages; typed index of tract names; original index; entries on lands patented up to 1768 plus one page of names, owners and acreages of lands patented in 1790; alienations to 1768. This is the Revenue Office counterpart (pp. 1-192) of Liber 26, and, from pp. 193-204 of Liber 28, pp. 192-106 [-206].

Liber 28—*Rent Roll Charles No. 3.* 47 pages; typed index of tract names; entries on lands patented up to 1768 plus additional rent rolls for the years 1769-1775 plus the names, owners and acreages of lands patented 1782-1790.

Liber 29—*Rent Roll Dorchester and Caroline No. 1.* 357 pages; typed index of tract names:
   (1) Additional annual rent rolls for Dorchester County between 1733 and 1764 (pp. 1-349); alienations to 1772.
   (2) Caroline County (pp. 350-357); record of lands patented 1782-1790.

Liber 30—*Rent Roll Dorchester No. 2.* 90 pages; typed index of tract names; contains additional rent rolls for Dorchester County from 1733 to 1746, comprising the first fourteen of the thirty-two additional rent rolls found in Liber 29; alienations to 1746.

Liber 31—*Rent Roll Dorchester No. 3.* 173 pages; typed index of tract names; contains additional rent rolls from 1764 to 1775 (pp. 1-159) and names, owners and acreages of lands patented between 1782 and 1790 (pp. 160-173); alienations to 1772.

Liber 32—*Rent Roll Frederick No. 1.* 234 pages; typed index of tract names; entries on lands patented to 1751; alienations to 1775.

Liber 33—*Rent Roll Frederick No. 2.* 80 pages; typed index of tract names; entries on lands patented to 1751 plus (pp. 81-103) names, owners and acreages of lands patented 1782-1790; alienations to 1770; original index. This is the Revenue Office counterpart of Liber 32, pp. 1-80.

Liber 34—*Rent Roll Frederick No. 3.* 179 pages; typed index of tract names; original index; entries on lands patented to 1759; alienations to 1775.

Liber 35—*Rent Roll Frederick No. 4.* Photostat of original; 271 pages; entries on lands patented to 1767; alienations to 1775; typed index of tract names; original has an index, not included in photostat copy.

Liber 36—*Rent Roll Frederick No. 5.* 241 pages; typed index of tract names; entries on lands patented to 1775 plus names, owners and acreages of lands patented 1783-1790; alienations to 1775.

Liber 37—*Rent Roll Kent No. 3.* 169 pages; typed index of tract names; contains (pp. 1-66) rent roll for Cecil County and (pp. 76-169) rent roll for Kent County. This is identical with Liber 25 in respect to arrangement and names of tracts. Alienations and the names of rent-payers are entirely lacking for the Cecil County rent roll, however, while the Kent County rent roll has the names of the rent-payers arranged alphabetically and though no alienations are included notations of resurveys are.

Liber 38—*Rent Roll Prince George's No. 1.* 234 pages; typed index of tract names; rent-roll entries of lands patented to 1756; alienations to 1775.

Liber 39—*Rent Roll Prince George's No. 2.* 234 pages; typed index of tract names; entries on lands patented to 1756; alienations to 1769. This is the Revenue Office counterpart of Liber 38.

Liber 40—*Rent Roll Prince George's No. 3.* 68 pages; typed index of tract names; alienation entries to 1769; title page: "Prince George's County Rent Roll 1757." This is the Revenue Office counterpart of Liber 41, pp. 1-69.

Liber 41—*Rent Roll Prince George's No. 4.* 105 pages; typed index of tract names; entries on lands patented to 1775, including not only the 1757 rent roll but additional rent rolls 1769-1775 and in addition, the names, owners and acreages of lands patented 1783-1788; title page: "Prince George's County Rent Roll Lib. No. 2 Anno 1757;" alienations to 1775.

Liber 42—*Rent Roll Queen Anne No. 4.* 104 pages; hand-written index; typed index of tract names; contains (pp. 1-102) additional rent rolls 1752-1775 and (pp. 103-4) names, owners and acreages of lands patented 1782-1790; alienations to 1772.

Liber 43—*Rent Roll St. Mary's No. 3.* 163 pages; typed index of tract names; pp. 1-151 are the Revenue Office counterpart of pp. 1-151 of Liber 44,4 pp. 152-158 contain rent-roll entries on lands patented 1768-69, pp. 159-163 contain names, owners and acreages of lands patented 1782-1790; alienations to 1768.

Liber 44—*Rent Roll St. Mary's No. 4.* 254 pages; typed index of tract names.

    (1) pp. 1-151; title page: "The Rent Roll of St. Mary's County;" entries on lands patented to 1768; alienations to 1775.

(2) pp. 152-254 (original paging 1-106); title page: "The Rent Roll of St. Mary's County to Michaelmass 1763;" entries on lands patented up to 1763, computation of total rent roll, list of manor tenants, index; no alienations.

Liber 45—*Rent Roll Somerset No. 3.* 237 pages; typed index of tract names; contains additional rent rolls of Somerset County 1735-1765; alienations to 1772.

Liber 46—*Rent Roll Somerset No. 4.* 67 pages; typed index of tract names; contains additional rent rolls of Somerset County 1766-1775 plus names, owners and acreages of lands patented 1782-1790; alienations to 1772.

Liber 47—*Rent Roll Talbot No. 3.* 126 pages; typed index of tract names; entries on lands patented to 1755; no alienations. Entries are arranged alphabetically according to the name of the person paying the rent.

Liber 48—*Rent Roll Worcester No. 1.* 169 pages; typed index of tract names; contains additional rent rolls of Worcester County 1743-1762; alienations to 1763.

Liber 49—*Rent Roll Worcester No. 2.* 125 pages; typed index of tract names; contains additional rent rolls 1763-1775 plus names, owners and acreages of lands patented 1782-1790; only one or two alienation entries.

DEBT BOOK SERIES

Liber 1—*Debt Book 1753, 54, 55, 56 Anne Arundel County.* Four small books bound together, each containing the list of persons owning property, the names of each piece of property and its rent and the total rent as paid in the years 1753, 1754, 1755, 1756. The 1753 debt book has 89 pages; 1754 has 82 pages; 1755 has 91 (not all numbered); 1756 has 72 pages and the entries, unlike the preceding books, are here arranged alphabetically by names of rent-payers.

Liber 2—*Debt Book 1757, 58, 59, 60, 61, 62, 63 Anne Arundel County.* Seven small books bound together, each containing entries as above. The 1757 debt book has 69 pages; 1758 has 55; 1759 has 80; 1760 has 71; 1761 has 62; 1762 has 65 and 1763 has 59 pages. All are arranged alphabetically by names of rent-payers.

Liber 3—*Debt Books 1764, 65, 66, 67, 68 Anne Arundel County.* Five small books bound together, each containing entries as above. The 1764 debt book has 64 pages; 1765 has 62 pages; 1766 has 63 pages; 1767 has 64 pages; 1768 has 66 pages. All are arranged alphabetically by names of rent-payers.

Liber   **4**—*Debt Books 1769, 70, 71, 74 Anne Arundel County.* Four small books bound together, each containing entries as above. The 1769 debt book has 74 pages; 1770 has 75 pages; 1771 has 86 and 1774 has 111 pages. All are arranged alphabetically by names of rent-payers.

Liber   **5**—*Debt Books 1754, 55, 56, 57 Baltimore County.* Four small books bound together, each containing entries as above. The 1754 debt book has 91 pages; 1755 has 82 pages; 1756 has 89 pages and 1757 has 81 pages. No alphabetical arrangement.

Liber   **6**—*Debt Books 1758, 59, 60, 61 Baltimore County.* Four small books bound together, each containing entries as above. The debt book for 1758 has 95 pages (the first two missing); 1759 has 86 pages and part of an index; 1760 has 106 pages (several of the last pages misbound); 1761 has 80 pages. No alphabetical arrangement.

Liber   **7**—*Debt Books 1762, 63, 64, 65 Baltimore County.* Four small books bound together, containing entries as above. The debt book for 1762 has 87 pages; 1763 has 89 pages; 1764 has 90 pages; 1765 has 94 pages. No alphabetical arrangement.

Liber   **8**—*Debt Books 1766, 1768 Baltimore County.* Two books bound together, containing entries as above. The debt book for 1766 has 97 pages, the one for 1768 has 112 pages. No alphabetical arrangement.

Liber   **9**—*Debt Books 1769, 70, 71 Baltimore County.* Three books bound together, each containing entries as above. The 1769 debt book has 124 pages, 1770 has 135 pages and 1771 has 131 pages (last one or two missing). The latter two of these three volumes have the entries arranged alphabetically by names of rent-payers.

Liber   **10**—*Debt Books 1753-58 Calvert County.* Six small volumes for the above-mentioned years, bound together, containing entries as above. The 1753 debt book has 45 pages; 1754 has 44 pages and part of an index; 1755, 1756, 1757 and 1758 each have 41 pages. No alphabetical arrangement.

Liber   **11**—*Debt Books 1761-68 Calvert County.* Eight small volumes for the above-mentioned years, bound together, containing entries as above. The debt book for 1761 has 37 pages and part of an index; 1762 has 34 pages; 1763 has 23 pages and part of an index; 1764 and 1765 each have 30 pages; 1766 has 27 pages and part of an index; 1767 has 20 pages; 1768 has 25 pages. With the exception of the first one, all of these volumes are arranged alphabetically by names of rent-payers.

Liber **12**—*Debt Books 1769-74 Calvert County.* Five small books for the years 1769, 1770, 1771, 1773, 1774 bound together, each containing entries as above. The debt books for 1769 and 1770 each have 29 pages; 1771 has 36 pages; 1773 has 40 pages; 1774 has 35 pages. Entries in all of these books are arranged alphabetically by names of rent-payers.

Liber **13**—*Debt Books 1753-56 Charles County.* Four small books bound together, each containing entries as above. The debt book for 1753 has 48 pages; 1754 has 103 pages; 1755 has 84 pages; 1756 has 87 pages. No alphabetical arrangement.

Liber **14**—*Debt Books 1757-61 Charles County.* Five books bound together, containing entries as above. The debt books for 1757 and 1758 each have 87 pages; 1759 has 60 pages; 1760 has 52 pages and part of an index; 1761 has 53 pages. No alphabetical arrangement.

Liber **15**—*Debt Books 1762-66 Charles County.* Five books bound together, each containing entries as above. The debt book for 1762 has 52 pages; 1763 has 54 pages; 1764 and 1765 each have 57 pages; 1766 has 60 pages. No alphabetical arrangement.

Liber **16**—*Debt Books 1767-71 Charles County.* Five books bound together, each containing entries as above. The debt book for 1767 has 60 pages, for 1768, 40 pages, for 1769, 41 pages, for 1770, 77 pages and for 1771, 55 pages. No alphabetical arrangement.

Liber **17**—*Debt Books 1772, 73, 74 Charles County.* Three books bound together, each containing entries as above. The debt book for 1772 has 75 pages, for 1773, 91 pages and for 1774, 70 pages. No alphabetical arrangement.

Liber **18**—*Debt Books 1734, 39, 49, 54 Cecil County.* Four books bound together, each containing entries as above. The debt book for 1734 has 102 pages; as originally numbered 1739 has 29 pages plus 15 additional lists of lands included in resurveys, etc.; 1749 has 42 pages; 1754 has

45 pages. Several pages are misbound. No alphabetical arrangement.

Liber 19—*Debt Books 1755, 57, 58, 60, 61, 66 Cecil County.* Six books bound together, each containing entries as above. The debt book for 1755 (here improperly labelled 1758) has 63 pages; the debt book for 1756 and 1757 has 27 pages; 1758 (here improperly labelled and inserted as 1755) has 60 pages. The 1760 debt book is mislabelled—the date is illegible—but it has the same arrangement and almost the identical entries as the 1734 debt book and does not include alienations beyond 1738, so is probably to be dated somewhere in the thirties. It has 66 pages. The debt book for 1761 has 25 pages; 1766 has 62 pages. All of these books are arranged alphabetically by names of rent-payers with the exception of the mislabelled "1760" one.

Liber 20—*Debt Books 1734, 37, 56 Dorchester County.* Three small books bound together, each containing entries as above. The debt book for 1734 has 136 pages; 1737 has 112 pages; 1756 has 160 pages. The 1756 debt book is arranged alphabetically by names of rent-payers, the other two are not.

Liber 21—*Debt Books 1758, 66, 67, 70 Dorchester County.* Four small books bound together, each containing entries as above. The debt book for 1758 has 129 pages; 1766 has 140 pages; 1767 has 134 pages; 1770 has 178 pages. All are arranged alphabetically by names of rent-payers.

Liber 22—*Debt Book 1753 Frederick County.* This debt book has 66 pages and an index. No alphabetical arrangement.

Liber 22—*Debt Book 1754-1757 Frederick County.* Three volumes bound together, each containing entries as above, for the years 1754, 1755 and 1756 plus a few entries of rents due in 1757 and paid in 1759. The debt book for 1754 has 101 pages and an index; 1755 has 112 pages; 1756 has 114 pages and includes the debt book for an additional rent roll, a separate list of lands lying on the west side of South Mountain, a list of entries of rents due in 1757 and an index. No alphabetical arrangement.

Liber 23—*Debt Books 1759-61 Frederick County.* Three books bound together, each containing entries as above. The debt book for 1759 has 108 pages plus 10 pages of entries on "Lands lying on the west side of the South Mountain" (the latter are mixed up, misbound and renumbered) and an index. The 1760 debt book has 102 pages, 1761 has 127 pages. The latter two volumes are arranged alphabetically by names of rent-payers, the first is not.

Liber 24—*Debt Books 1762-1763-1766 Frederick County.* Three books bound together, each containing entries as above. The debt book for 1762 has 196 pages; 1763 has 205 pages; 1766 has 138 pages, the first two missing. All these volumes are arranged alphabetically by names of rent-payers.

Liber 25—*Debt Book 1768-70 Frederick County.* Three books bound together, each containing entries as above. The debt book for 1768 has 202 pages, the first page missing; 1769 has 161 pages; 1770 has 145 pages. All these volumes are arranged alphabetically by names of rent-payers.

Liber 26—*Debt Books 1771-73 Frederick County.* Three books bound together, each containing entries as above. The debt book for 1771 has 181 pages, the first eight pages missing; 1772 has 187 pages; 1773 has 195 pages. All are arranged alphabetically by names of rent-payers.

Liber 27—*Debt Books 1733, 34, 35 Kent County.* Six small books bound together, each containing entries as above. The debt book for 1733 has 88 pages; the two parts of the 1734 debt book have 56 and 62 pages respectively; the three parts of the 1735 debt book have 86, 61 and 58 pages respectively. No alphabetical arrangement.

Liber 28—*Debt Books 1736-40 Kent County.* Five books bound together, each containing entries as above. The debt book for 1736 has 74 pages; 1737 has 118 pages; 1738 has 60 pages and part of an index; 1739 has 48 pages; 1740 has 50 pages and part of an index. No alphabetical arrangement.

Liber 29—*Debt Books 1741-43 Kent County.* Three books bound together, each containing entries as above. The 1741 debt book has 79 pages; 1742 has 57 pages; 1743 has 60 pages. No alphabetical arrangement.

Liber 30—*Debt Books 1744, 47, 52, 53 Kent County.* Four books bound together, each containing entries as above. The 1744 debt book has 71 pages, the first page missing; 1747 has 102 pages; 1752 has 132 pages; 1753 has 109 pages. The latter two volumes are arranged alphabetically by names of rent-payers, the first two are not.

Liber 31—*Debt Books 1754, 56, 57 Kent County.* Three books bound together, each containing entries as above. The 1754 debt book has 128 pages; 1756 has 107 pages; 1757 has 122 pages. All these books are arranged alphabetically by names of rent-payers.

Liber 32—*Debt Books 1760, 69 Kent County.* Two books bound together, each containing entries as above. The debt book for 1760 has 70 pages plus an additional short list; 1769 has 157 pages plus a short additional list. These are both arranged alphabetically by names of rent-payers.

Liber 33—*Debt Books 1753-54, 55, 56, 58 Prince George's County.* Five books bound together, each containing entries as above. The 1753 debt book has 64 pages; 1754 has 50 pages; 1755 has 84 pages; 1756 has 61 pages; 1758 has 48 pages. No alphabetical arrangement.

Liber 34—*Debt Books 1759 to 1765 Prince George's County.* Seven books bound together, each containing entries as above. The 1759 debt book has 65 pages; 1760 has 48 pages; 1761 has 64 pages; 1762 has 64 pages; 1763-4 has 33 pages and an index; 1765 has 31 pages and an index. No alphabetical arrangement.

Liber 35—*Debt Books 1766-67-68-69-71-72 Prince George's County.* Six books bound together, each containing entries as above. The 1766 debt book has 33 pages; 1767, 1768 and 1769 each have 33 pages and part of an index; 1771 has 33 pages; 1772 has 36 pages. No alphabetical arrangement.

Liber 36—*Debt Books 1734-1747-1754-1756-1757 Queen Anne's County.* Five books bound together, each containing entries as above. The debt book for 1734 has 100 pages plus some additional short lists; 1747 has 146 pages, the first page missing; 1754 has 116 pages; 1756 has 142 pages; 1757 has 73 pages. The last three of these books are arranged alphabetically by names of rent-payers, the first two are not.

Liber 37—*Debt Books 1756-58 Queen Anne County.* Three books bound together, containing entries as above. The debt book labelled 1756 has no title date but it was received in February 1756, so it would seem to be the 1756 debt book. It has 106 pages. The debt book labelled 1757 has no title date but is marked as being the debt book due in 1758, hence would seem to be the 1758 debt book. It has 152 pages. The volume labelled the 1758 debt book is wrongly titled as it consists of a collection of lists of defective rents from the year 1745. It has 38 pages. Entries in all these volumes are arranged alphabetically by names of rent-payers.

Liber 38—*Debt Books 1758-1763-1765-1766-1767-1769-1775 Queen Anne's County.* Seven books covering the above-mentioned years, bound together, each containing entries as above. The 1758 debt book has 79 pages; 1763 has 80 pages; 1765 has 68 pages; 1766 has 124 pages; 1767 has 77 pages; 1769 has 68 pages; 1775 has 44 pages. The entries in all these books are arranged alphabetically by names of rent-payers.

Liber 39—*Debt Books 1753-1754-1755-1756-1757-1758 Saint Mary's County.* Six books bound together, each containing entries as above. The debt book for 1753 has 49 pages; 1754, 1755 and 1756 each have 50 pages and part of an index; 1757 has 51 pages; 1758 has 49 pages. No alphabetical arrangement.

Liber 40—*Debt Books 1759, 60, 61, 62, 63, 64, 65, 66 Saint Mary's County.* Eight small books bound together, each containing entries as above. The 1759 debt book has 42 pages and an additional rent-roll list of entries; 1760 has 47 pages; 1761 has 53 pages; 1762 has 50 pages; 1763 has 47 pages; 1764 has 45 pages; 1765 and 1766 each have 45 pages. No alphabetical arrangement.

Liber 41—*Debt Books 1767-74 Saint Mary's County.* Seven books for the above-mentioned years except 1772, bound together, containing entries as above. The 1767 debt book has 42 pages, 1768 has 30 pages, 1769 has 31 pages, 1770 has 44 pages, 1771 has 39 pages, 1773 has 55 pages, 1774 has 58 pages. No alphabetical arrangement.

Liber 42—*Debt Books 1733-34 Somerset County.* Two books bound together, each containing entries as above. The debt book for 1733 has 217 pages, 1734 has 132 pages. Though the latter is labelled 1734, comparison with the rent roll would seem to date it after 1736. No alphabetical arrangement.

Liber 43—*Debt Books 1735-48 Somerset County.* Three books, for the years 1735, 1745 and 1748, bound together, each containing entries as above. The debt book for 1735 has 196 regularly numbered pages plus some 12 additional pages of entries including pages numbered as high as 249. It also has part of an index. The debt book for 1745 has 206 pages, 1748 has 232 pages. No alphabetical arrangement.

Liber   44—*Debt· Books 1756-61 Worcester County.* Five books bound together, each containing entries as above. The 1756 debt book has 198 pages, 1757-58 (designated on its first page as being for 1756, 1757, 1758) has 203 pages, 1759 has 134 pages, 1760 has 69 pages, 1761 has 50 pages. In all these books the entries are arranged alphabetically by names of rent-payers.

Liber   45—*Debt Books 1759-1761-1764-1768-1769-1774 Somerset County.* Six books bound together, each containing entries as above. The 1759 debt book has 141 pages, 1761 has 119 pages, 1764 has 56 pages, 1768 has 75 pages, 1769 has 81 pages, 1774 has 78 pages. In all these books the entries are arranged alphabetically by names of rent-payers.

Liber   46—*Debt Books 1733-44 Talbot County.* Three books, for the years 1733, 1738 and 1744, bound together, each containing entries as above. The 1733 debt book has 118 pages, 1738 has 101 pages, 1744 (only a pencilled date mark on this book) has 56 pages. No alphabetical arrangement.

Liber 47-48—*Debt Books 1739-48 Talbot County.* Two books, for the years 1739 and 1748, bound together. The volume for 1739 is entitled "Abstract from Rent Roll to be remark't and possessors of each Tract Charged" and is not in the usual debt book form, the entries being listed under the names of the tracts of land and alienations noted as in a rent roll. It has 150 pages. The 1748 debt book has 65 pages. No alphabetical arrangement.

Liber   49—*Debt Books 1756-61 Talbot County.* Four books for the above-mentioned years excepting 1760, bound together, each containing entries as above. The debt book labelled "1756" has no authentic date mark and is apparently of a later date, possibly 1760. It has 91 pages. The 1757-58 debt book has "1756, 1757, 1758" marked on its cover. It has 64 pages. The 1759 debt book has 72 pages and the 1761 debt book has 106 pages. In all these books the entries are arranged alphabetically by names of rent-payers.

Liber   50—*Debt Books 1766-72 Talbot County.* Six books for the above years excepting 1767, bound together, each containing entries as above. The debt book for 1766 has 82 pages, 1768 has 85 pages, 1769 has 73 pages plus a few additional rent roll entries, 1770 has 54 pages, 1771 has 65 pages, 1772 has 72 pages. All these books have the entries arranged alphabetically by names of rent-payers.

Liber **51**—*Debt Books 1745-1755 Somerset County.* Two debt books for the years 1745 and 1755, bound together, each containing entries as above. The debt book labelled "1745" has no authentic date mark; it has 120 pages; 1755 has 209 pages plus various additional short lists of lands and part of an index. The first of these volumes is arranged alphabetically by names of rent-payers, the second is not.

Liber **52**—*Debt Books 1745-1755 Worcester County.* Two debt books for the years 1745 and 1755, bound together, each containing entries as above. The 1745 debt book has 177 pages, 1755 has 205 pages plus various additional lists of lands. No alphabetical arrangement.

Liber **53**—*Debt Books 1762-1768-1769-1771-1774 Worcester County.* Five books for the above-mentioned years, bound together, each containing entries as above. The debt book for 1762 has 115 pages; 1768 has 42 pages; 1769 has 146 pages plus five pages of additional rent roll entries; 1771 has 40 pages, the first four missing; 1774 has 139 pages. All these volumes have the entries arranged alphabetically by names of rent-payers.

Liber **54**—*Debt Books Additional for Worcester, Somerset, Talbot, Cecil, Dorchester, Kent.* Eight small volumes bound together, each containing short debt books ranging in date from 1734 to 1758 for additional rent rolls of Cecil, Kent, Dorchester, Talbot, Worcester and Somerset Counties. The latter two counties have two volumes and the other one volume each. No alphabetical arrangement.[87]

---

[87] In addition to the above numbered series of debt books, the Land Office also has three unbound debt books, one, a duplicate of the Queen Anne's Debt Book for 1734 and the other two, undated, from Cecil County.

VOLUME INDEXES[88]

General Index to Cer. & Pat. 1658 to 1694—No. 2.
General Index to Cer. & Pat. 1686 to 1776—No. 3.
General Index to Patents 1680 to 1759—No. 5.
General Index to Patents 1759 to 1777—No. 6.

General Index to Warrants & Assignments Earliest to 1688—No. 1.
General Index Warrants 1679 to 1751—No. 1.
General Index Warrants 1751 to 1764—No. 2.
General Index Warrants 1764 to 1774—No. 3.
General Index Warrants 1774 to 1803—No. 4.

Index to Debt Books—1753-1774—Dorchester, Somerset and Worcester Counties.
Index to Debt Books—1753-1775—Queen Anne's, Kent, Talbot and Cecil Counties.
Index to Debt Books—1753-1774—St. Mary's and Charles Counties.
Index to Debt Books—1753-1774—Frederick County.
Index to Debt Books—1753-1772—Calvert and Prince George's Counties.
Index to Debt Books—1754-1771—Baltimore County.
Index to Additional Debt Books Eastern Shores, includes returns from Worcester, Dorchester, Somerset, Cecil, Kent and Talbot—1734-1759.
General Index to the Debt Books of Anne Arundel County 1753-

[88] In addition to the volume indexes included in the following list, the Land Office has a modern card-index file of names covering these records with the exception of the *Proprietary Leases*.

LAND OFFICE RECORDS, 1680

"A List of the Records of Lands taken out of the Secretary's Office for which John Llewellin Register Appointed for the Land Office passed his Receipt the 7th April Anno 1680; according to his Lordships orders of the 3rd Ditto in the words underneath the Said List—

Lib	A	Provinciall & Lands 1646 to 1650
	B	The same and one Alphabett to both bookes
	F	Records for Lands from 1640 to 1643
	H	Entry of Lands from 1650 to 1655
	I&K	Burles 2 Bookes of Rights from 1649 to 1657
	L	Lands from 1656 to 1657
	P	Booke of Rights & Warrants 1660
	Q	Lands 1658
	R	Lands 1659
	X	Lands from 1661 to 1663
	AA	Lands 1663
	CC	Lands 1664 & 1665
	DD	Lands 1665
	EE	Lands 1665 & 1666
	FF	Lands 1667
	GG	Lands 1667 & 1668
	HH	Lands 1668 & 1669
	JJ	Lands 1669
	RM	Lands at the WhoreKill 1670
	WT	Lands 1670 71 72
	MM	Lands 1672 73 74 75 76 77
	LL	Lands 1673 74 75 76 77 78
		Several Bundles of Certificates
	KK	Lands 1670
	WC	Lands 1675 76 77 78 79 80
	WC	No. 2—Lands 1679 80
	D	Booke of Instructions
	HH	Councill Booke 1656
	JJ	Councill Booke 1670
	CB	Commissions from the Lord Proprietor
	RR	Councill Booke 1671 to 1673
		Conditions of Plantations

You are desired and hereby required to Deliver into the Custody of John Llewellin to be kept at the State house the severall Bookes and Papers in your Office relateing to the business of Lands according to the within written List, and what other Bookes and papers you have any waies relateing thereunto for which this shall be your Sufficient order from

C: Baltimore

To the Honorable William Calvert Esquire Principall Secretary of this Province or his Chiefe Clark these./"

— — Warrants 3, 3

PREROGATIVE COURT RECORDS

OF

MARYLAND

By

GUST SKORDAS

The probate court of Maryland for the greater part of the colonial period was called the Prerogative Court. Many of the features of the court, notably the terminology, were borrowed from the English Prerogative Court. Unlike the English court which was ecclesiastical, the Maryland court remained a civil court throughout its existence, although there were several attempts to put it under the control of the Bishop of London. The attempt which came closest to succeeding was made soon after Maryland became a royal colony. At that time, a strong effort was being made to establish the Church of England in the Colony. The attitude of the colonists in the matter of the probate office and toward religion in general was expressed by the members of the Upper House of the Assembly when they unanimously agreed, on October 18, 1694, "That a Suffragan Bishop or Comissary Deputed by & invested with such Eccliasticall Authority & power by the Right Reverend Father in God The Rt Honoble the Lord Bishop of London as to his wisdom shall seem most Expedient for the Better setling & Regulateing all matters Relateing to Churches and Churchmen which are or shall be Establisht by God Almightys providence & his paternall care in this province will be most convenient & Necessary, But wee doe further represent unto the said Burgesses of Assembly That the Comissary's office in the Nature of it & by the Just & Honest profits & advantages accruing unto it is a most sutable Employment and a Valuable Encouragement for such Suffragan Bishop or Comissary so to be Deputed by his Lsp: without any charge to be laid upon this province.

"First because that Office being Judiciall & of great importance & Trust in this province in quieting & secureing to the Right owners all Estates of persons Dying Testate or Intestate & for preserveing the fortunes of all the Orphans of Maryland cannot well be Executed but by a person of Integrity and Capacity resideing among us. And Secondly that being a Judiciall office of an Ecclesiasticall nature it ought to be performed by a person Qualifyed by his knowledge in the Civill Law and may also properly appertain to the same person if he shall have taken any degrees in the Study of Divinity."[1]

---

[1] *Arch. Md.*, XIX, 92.

Two years later, the Assembly passed a law bestowing the office of Commissary General upon the "Divine or Commissary" expected from the Bishop of London. The law required the Governor upon the arrival here and application by the "said Divine" to grant and confirm the office to him. It was stipulated, however, that he must be a resident of the Province and not exercise the office by deputy or representative.[2] On October 3, 1698, the Bishop of London issued a commission to Thomas Bray, D.D., as Commissary for the Province of Maryland.[3] Eventually the long-awaited Commissary did arrive. On May 4, 1700, Dr. Bray appeared before the Governor and Council in support of Edward Dorsey's petition for the remission of a fine.[4] But on June 27, 1700, the Governor announced to his council that Dr. Bray having gone to England he, the Governor, had conferred the Commissary's Office upon Thomas Brooke, one of the Council. At the same time, he asserted he was willing that upon the return of Bray or "any other qualified person sent in by the right Reverend the Lord Bishop of London" he "should enjoy that office."[5] Bray does not appear in the records of the Prerogative Court at all, probably because he confined his attention to strictly religious problems and did not apply for the office of Commissary General as required by the law of 1696. In any case neither Bray nor any other Commissary returned to take advantage of the Governor's offer.[6]

ORIGIN AND EARLY DEVELOPMENT OF THE PREROGATIVE COURT

The Prerogative Court did not spring into existence, a full-fledged court. Like the other institutions of the Province, it was the product of a gradual evolution, influenced by the customs of the home country and the needs of the new. Its origin can be traced back to the Charter granted to Lord Baltimore in 1632. In it, he was given complete control over the colony, including authority in religious matters comparable to that of the Bishop of Durham.

[2] *Ibid.*, XXXVIII, 92.

[3] *Ibid.*, XXV, 11.

[4] *Ibid.*, XXIV, 62.

[5] *Ibid.*, XXV, 95.

[6] For a more thorough discussion of the religious aspects of the office of commissary general and of the efforts to place it under the control of the church, see Edith E. MacQueen, "The Commissary in Colonial Maryland" (*Md. Hist. Mag.*, XXV, 190-206).

This, of course, included control over probate matters. Poor communications made it impractical for the Lord Proprietary to govern the colony from England; therefore he found it necessary to appoint a deputy to govern the colony and look after his interests in it. The commission he issued to his brother, Leonard Calvert, on April 15, 1637, is the earliest such appointment found in the records of the colony. Leonard was named Lieutenant General, as the Governor was then called, and placed in charge of all phases of the government.[7] A Council was named to advise and assist him. John Lewger, one of the members of the Council, was also designated as Secretary of the Province and made responsible for the keeping and recording of the acts and proceedings of the Lieutenant General and his Council. On January 20, 1637[8],[8] the Governor issued a commission assigning additional duties to Lewger. Besides being named "Conservator of the Peace within the County of St. Maries", Lewger was also appointed Commissioner "in causes testamentary, to prove the last wills and testaments of persons deceased, and to grant admraōn of the estates of persons dying intestate within our said Province and to take inventaries and accompts and the same to record, and to give discharges thereupon; and to minister an oath to any person or persons witnesse or witnesses exequutors or admrātors as often as there shall be cause."[9]

A few years later, on August 12, 1641, "An Act For Causes Testamentary" was passed. It provided the "Lieutent. Generall or in his absence his Deputie or otherwise the first Counsellour resident in the County shall prove Wills and Grant Administracōns & exercise all Temporal jurisdictions to Testamentary causes appertayning". He was to proceed "according to the Law or lawdable usage of England....& where the same is uncertain or doubtful then according to equity & good concience."[10] In practice, Secretary Lewger continued to do most of the work. On September 5, 1642, when Calvert renewed Lewger's commission as Secretary of the

[7] Arch. Md., III, 49.

[8] Long after Catholic Europe had adopted the Gregorian calendar which we now use, England retained the Julian calendar, refusing to change unitl 1752. In this calendar, the year started on March 25, the period from January 1 through March 24 being considered part of the previous year. In order to bring dates falling within this period into proper perspective, the year according to the Gregorian calendar has been inserted in brackets after such dates.

[9] Arch. Md., III, 60.

[10] Ibid., I, 108.

Province, he also made him "Judge of all Causes Testamentary & Matrimoniall".[11] The linking of probate and matrimonial matters was obviously influenced by the practice in England.

In spite of the confusion created by Ingle's Rebellion and the seizure of the government by the Parliamentary Commissioners, it appears that the person occupying the position of Secretary of the Province continued to have jurisdiction over probate matters until 1673. Every Secretary's commission found in the records of the Province before then includes this responsibility. However, some of the governors took an active interest in the office. Philip and Charles Calvert, especially, are often mentioned in the records as having proved a will, granted letters of administration or performed some similar duty.

Although the chief officer for probate matters had been called a judge as early as 1642,[12] he did not begin to preside over a court until much later. The first style of court appeared in the records on July 30, 1670 while William Calvert was Secretary.[13] About the same time, the Court began to try libels, issue citations, and perform other duties of a judicial nature. But it was not until Sir William Talbot became Secretary that the Prerogative Court may be said to have been formally established. His commission, which was issued by Lord Baltimore on August 7, 1670, included the usual powers of a Secretary. In addition he was given "full Power and Authority to issue out Commissions and process in our name and to hear Sentence and declare all matters touching wills Administrations and Inventories and also the Incidents Emergencies and dependencies thereupon and to make and appoint Registers & other Officers in relation to the Probate of wills and Granting of Administrations in all Counties and places within our said Province."[14] It was on May 19, 1671, during his term of office

---

[11] *Ibid.*, III, 116. By this time, the Secretary was performing an infinite number of duties. In addition to the probate and matrimonial duties already mentioned, the commission cited above made him "principall officer and keeper of the acts and proceeding of us [Lord Proprietary] and of o^r Lieutent Grall and Counsell. . . , and for the entring and recording of all grants. . . . of any lands or offices within o^r said Province of Maryland, and for the entring and recording of all other matters, acts and things" concerning the Province. He was also made "Collector and Receivor of all our rents revenues and customes."

[12] *Ibid.*, I, 154.

[13] *Testamentary Proceedings* 4A, 11.

[14] *Arch. Md.*, V, 70.

that the name, "Prerogative Court," was used in the records of the Court for the first time.[15]

COMMISSARY GENERAL

Talbot was the last Secretary to have jurisdiction in probate matters. When Philip Calvert received a commission as Chancellor and "Judge or Commissary Generall for Probate of wills" on November 20, 1672, the office was divorced from that of the Secretary forever.[16] Calvert apparently did not like the term "Prerogative Court," because from the time he was sworn in on April 24, 1673 until his death in 1682, it was never used in the records of the Court. A few years after his death, the term reappeared in the records and was used continuously until the end of the Court. Col. Henry Darnall and Col. William Digges succeeded Philip Calvert,[17] both in his capacity as Commissary General and as Chancellor. But with the appointment of Kenelm Cheseldyn, in 1693, the Commissary General became established as an officer in his own right. In a few years, the office became one of the most lucrative in the Colony and was eagerly sought after. It was not unusual for two or three men to hold the office together and in 1722 four judges were named in the same commission.[18] Usually, however, only one judge was appointed. The duties of the Commissary General were similar to those of the Secretary in so far as he had been concerned with probate matters. But as time passed the Commissaries tended to confine their attention mainly to the hearing of disputes and to leave the ordinary probate work of the Court to the Chief Clerk and Register.

CHIEF CLERK AND REGISTER

The office of Chief Clerk and Register of the Prerogative Court appears to have had its origin in the office of "Clerke of the Secretaryes Office and the provinciall Courts." The first such clerk to appear in the records of the Province is William Bretton, who was serving in this capacity as early as 1647.[19]

---

[15] *Testamentary Proceedings* 4A, 11.
[16] *Ibid.*, 5, 425.
[17] *Ibid.*, 13, flyleaf.
[18] *Ibid.*, 26, 71.
[19] *Arch. Md.*, IV, 324.

He may have been preceded by other clerks, but the commissions of the early clerks were not often recorded and it is difficult to trace them. The commission issued by Governor Charles Calvert to John Blomfield on May 5, 1669, as "Chief Clerk of the Secretaries Office of the Provincial Court and Council and of the Custody and keeping of the lesser Seal Records" was the first such commission to be recorded. The accompanying instructions empowered him to sign letters of administration, probate wills and sign warrants to appraisers.[20]

After the offices of Secretary and Commissary General were separated in 1673, each officer had his own clerk or clerks. As long as Philip Calvert was Commissary General, his clerk did little more than record the proceedings of the Court and the instruments filed with it. But after Calvert's death, the duties of the clerk increased steadily and he was frequently referred to as the Register of the Prerogative Court. For example, in 1685 the proceedings of the Court reveal that James Cullen "was appointed by the Judges to be Register of this Court & Clerke of the Office for probat of wills . . ."[21] The title varied considerably in subsequent appointments, but the version most commonly used was "Chief Clerk and Register of the Prerogative Court".

By 1700, the Register had acquired a deputy and was performing most of the routine work of the Court. The commissaries or judges held court at least every two months. While in session, they heard disputes and reviewed the work done by the Register since the last session. A typical court term, as found in the proceedings of the Prerogative Court, began with the style of court which gave the date, place and names of the commissaries present. This was followed by court orders, citations, attachments, etc. Then the docket of cases was heard and decided or continued as in any other court. Finally, the judges passed on accounts which had been allowed by the Register and adjourned until the next term. Between terms of court it is evident that the Prerogative Office remained open continuously, for there are almost daily entries in the proceedings. The entries consist largely of returns of the Deputy Commissaries for the various counties, but there are also entries regarding instruments which were brought directly to the office.

[20] *Ibid.*, V, 49-52.
[21] *Testamentary Proceedings* 13, 197.

LEGAL BACKGROUND OF THE PREROGATIVE COURT

Throughout the colonial period the General Assembly frequently concerned itself with probate matters, especially the protection of orphans' estates. In 1681, an Act entitled "An act for the better Admstracōn of Justice in probate of Wills, granting Admstracōns Recovery of Legacy & secureing fillial porcōns" was passed.[22] This Act may well be called the basic law of the Prerogative Court; for, with one important exception, none of the laws passed subsequently made any great change either in the organization or procedure of the Court. It required the Judge or Commissary General to "hold his court once in Two Months att the Least or oftner as the Case shall Requier." He was to proceed in all testamentary causes according to the Laws of England if pleaded before him except "in such cases as shall in this Act be Limited or shall heereafter bee Limited by Act of Assembly of this Province, as utterly impracticable in this Province." It was made lawful for the Judge to prove "any Last Will in this Province even though itt Concerne Title to Land any Law useage or Custome of the Kingdome of England to the Contrary Notwithstanding." Executors and administrators were to account for the estate within twelve months after administration was committed. The care of orphans' estates and choice of guardians was left to the county courts, but very elaborate and detailed regulations were prescribed by the law; the theory being that local authorities, being better acquainted with the individuals concerned and in the same locality where the estate was, could do a better job of protecting the interests of the orphans. Finally the right of appeal from the decision of the Commissary General which had been established in the commission issued to Philip Calvert in 1672 was confirmed, provided that the appellant enter his appeal before the Commissary within 15 days of the sentence and within 15 more days petition the Lord Proprietary or his Lieutenant to examine or appoint someone to examine the sentence of the Commissary. This law was renewed by acts passed in 1692,[23] 1699,[24] and 1715[25] which contained substantially the same provisions, but did vary in detail.

---

[22] *Arch. Md.*, VII, 195.

[23] *Ibid.*, XIII, 430.

[24] *Ibid.*, XXII, 533.

[25] *Ibid.*, XXX, 331.

DEPUTY COMMISSARY

The only significant change in the Prerogative Court after the passage of the above law was the establishment of the office of Deputy Commissary. The difficulties of travel in the newly settled colony imposed a severe hardship on the executors or administrators of estates located at any distance from the capital of the Province. Very early in the history of the probate office, it became customary to issue a special warrant or commission to some reliable person, quite often a justice of the county court, authorizing him to perform a specific duty in a specific case. For example, in 1642, a commission was issued to George Binks empowering him to administer the oath of appraisers to Thomas Greene and Nathan Pope who had been appointed appraisers of the estate of John Cockshott.[26] Commissions were also issued authorizing persons to probate wills and swear administrators. None of these commissions were of a general nature. By 1692, the number of commissions being issued had increased to such an extent that the Commissary General was authorized by law to "appoint some able and sufficient person of good repute and a freeholder in every respective County in this Province, to take the probate of any last will or Testament." He was also to grant letters of administration and letters testamentary and swear administrators and appraisers. If any dispute arose, it was to be decided by the Commissary General.[27] As a result of this act, a commission to a Deputy Commissary or Agent for each county was issued on August 9, 1692.[28] As time passed, the powers of the Deputy Commissaries tended to increase. The law of 1715 even authorized them to allow the accounts of estates valued at less than ·50 pounds sterling, provided there was no controversy. Where an estate exceeded 50 pounds, the Commissary General often reverted to the early practice of issuing a special commission allowing the Deputy Commissary to pass the account.

When a will, inventory or account was brought into the office of a Deputy Commissary, he took whatever action was necessary and recorded the instrument in his own books. Periodically he would send or deliver the papers filed in his office and a return of his proceedings in each case to the Prerogative Office, where the wills, inventories and accounts were again recorded and the returns of pro-

---

[26] *Ibid.*, IV, 72.
[27] *Ibid.*, XIII, 430.
[28] *Testamentary Proceedings* 14A, 3

ceedings entered in the Testamentary Proceedings.[29] Only in Anne Arundel County did this procedure vary. The Prerogative Court was located in Annapolis, the county seat, and therefore it was pointless for the Deputy Commissary to keep a duplicate set of records; particularly, since the Register of the Court was almost invariably appointed Deputy Commissary for Anne Arundel County also.[30] Therefore, the proceedings for this county were entered directly into the records of the Prerogative Court. Except for Anne Arundel County and the proceedings of the Court itself, the records of the Prerogative Court were duplicated by the records of the Deputy Commissaries. Naturally there were some discrepancies. Due to accident, carelessness or other causes, instruments may sometimes be found in one set which do not appear in the other.

HISTORY OF THE RECORDS OF THE PREROGATIVE COURT

The Constitution of 1776 provided for the appointment of a Register of Wills in each county and thus by implication abolished the Prerogative Court. Chapter 8 of the Laws of April 1777 carried out the intent of the Constitution by abolishing the Court and providing for the appointment of an Orphans' Court and a Register of Wills in each county to replace it.[31] The records of the Deputy Commissaries were passed on to the Registers of Wills. The records of the Prerogative Court were placed in the care and custody of the Register of Wills for Prince George's County. Annapolis being the provincial capital and one of the most important cities in the colonies, it was deemed safer to deposit the records elsewhere while the War lasted. But a few months later, Elie Vallette, Register of Wills for Anne Arundel County and previously Register of the Pre-

---

[29] In 1705, Humphrey Hubbard, Deputy Commissary of Dorchester County was carrying certain wills, inventories, accounts and other papers across the bay to the Commissary General's Office when his boat caught fire and sank, causing the papers to be lost. Fortunately, they had been copied into the Deputy Commissary's records before he left. A law was passed providing that copies of the lost papers taken from Hubbard's books be recorded in the Commissary General's Office. The law further provided that the copies be accepted as originals for all practical purposes. The copies were recorded in full in *Testamentary Proceedings* 19c, pages 150-176.

[30] There were only two exceptions to this custom. John Beale and Michael Macnemara served as Deputy Commissaries for Anne Arundel County during the period, 1719-1744, when the position of Register was occupied by other men.

[31] Hall of Records, *Catalogue of Archival Material*, p. 123.

rogative Court for the last thirteen years of its existence, submitted a memorial to the General Assembly. After stressing his own familiarity with the records and pointing out that the considerable unfinished business of the Court necessitated frequent reference to the records, he requested that they be returned to his custody. Accordingly, an act was passed requiring him to remove the records of the Court from Upper Marlboro to some safe place in Anne Arundel County at least nine miles from Annapolis.[32] He was ordered to hire a room in which to house them and to keep them stored in chests or trunks so that they might readily be moved if the Governor and Council so ordered. Since Vallette was so anxious to obtain the records, it seems reasonable to assume that he fulfilled the requirements of the law although no clue as to the location of the storage place can be found. In any case, on November 27, 1778, the Governor and Council ordered "that all the Books and Papers belonging to the Commissaries Office, be removed to the City of Annapolis under the care of the Register of Wills for Anne Arundel County,"[33] whose office at that time was located in the State House.

A few months later, in March 1779, a law was passed ordering that the Prerogative Court Papers dating from 1760 and belonging to estates which had not been finally settled be sorted and packed and delivered to the several Registers of Wills.[34] The rest of the papers were similarly distributed in 1783 when the officer having custody of them was ordered to record all unrecorded original papers and sort out, list and pack all original papers for each county.[35] Then he was to notify the Registers to send for them. As a result, the original papers of the Prerogative Court have since then been located in the offices of the Registers of Wills for the various counties.

The volumes had meanwhile remained in the custody of the Register of Wills for Anne Arundel County. In 1823, a resolution of the General Assembly authorized him to remove the records to his "fireproof office in the courthouse of Anne Arundel County."[36] There the records remained until 1904, when the Register was directed by law to deliver all the records and indexes of the Prerogative Court

---

[32] *Proceedings of the House of Delegates*, 1777, f. 292-293; *Recorded Laws of Maryland, Liber G. R. No. 1*, 1777-1778, f. 8 (June 1777, ch. 9).
[33] *Arch. Md.*, XXI, 255.
[34] Kilty, *Laws of Md.*, March 1779, ch. 15.
[35] Hanson, *Laws of Md.*, April 1783, ch. 9.
[36] *Laws of Md.*, 1822, Res. No. 44.

to the Commissioner of the Land Office, who had recently moved into his quarters in the new Court of Appeals building.[37] In June 1935, the Commissioner of the Land Office moved into the newly-erected Hall of Records building taking the records with him. A few months later, in December 1935, he transferred the Prerogative Court records to the custody of the Hall of Records Commission, where they now remain.

EFFORTS FOR THE PRESERVATION OF THE RECORDS

With the possible exception of the land records, no set of Maryland records had received more attention than those of the Prerogative Court. Since adequate repair facilities were not developed until very recently, earlier efforts toward preservation of the records consisted mainly of transcribing damaged pages or whole volumes and replacing worn bindings. As early as 1716, the General Assembly passed a law appointing several commissioners to examine and have repaired the records of the Province.[38] By virtue of this law, a good many of the records in the Commissary General's Office were rebound or given other attention. In a number of instances, two or more of the old libers were bound together, probably in the interest of economy. A committee of both houses of the Assembly was appointed in 1728 to inspect the work done by the commissioners. The report of the committee listing the volumes repaired and showing what was done to them was entered in the proceedings of the Lower House.[39]

Another extensive repair project was carried out in 1834, when the General Assembly authorized the Register of Wills for Anne Arundel County to have transcribed and rebound any of the provincial records in his office.[40] A similar law was passed in 1874 authorizing further repair work on the Prerogative Court records.[41]

Soon after the records were transfered to the Land Office, the legislature appropriated $6,000 for the restoration of State records.[42] As a result of this law, the entire set of Prerogative Court records was rebound, each series in a distinctive color. In addition, four

[37] Hall of Records, *Catalogue of Archival Material*, p. 53.
[38] Bacon's *Laws*, 1716, ch. 1.
[39] *Arch. Md.*, XXXVI, 236.
[40] *Laws of Md.*, 1834, ch. 147.
[41] *Ibid.*, 1874, ch. 381.
[42] *Ibid.*, 1908, ch. 606.

volumes of wills were transcribed in full.   In 1912, the Land Office
purchased a Photostat camera and adopted the policy of withdrawing
from circulation original volumes which had begun to deteriorate
and replacing them with bound photostat copies.   A number of
volumes were so treated.   But since 1935 when the records were
transferred to the Hall of Records, it has been possible to send
the original itself to a well-equipped repair department for such
treatment as is deemed necessary.   Ordinarily, the whole volume is
repaired and rebound.   A list of the volumes repaired is published
in the annual reports of the Archivist.

In the course of all this repair and rebinding, the original arrangement of the records has been considerably disrupted.   More-
over the system used for identifying the individual libers has also
been changed, partly because many of the libers had lost their
identity by being combined with other libers.   Before the present
system of numbered series was adopted, letters of the alphabet,
numbers and initials of the commissaries general or of the registers
had all been used at various times to identify the libers.   In the
lists below the old liber will be given immediately after the present
liber number.   The original liber numbers or letters are still found
on the flyleaves or elsewhere in many of the volumes.   Otherwise
they have been determined by referring to lists of the records made
in 1673,[43] 1687,[44] 1699[45] and 1776[46] and to the report of the committee of 1728.   The lists below will also indicate the existence of
handwritten or photostat copies, except in the case of the Proprietary Records which have already been fully analyzed in the "Calendar of State Archives" published in Volume I of the *Archives of
Maryland.*   Unless a definite statement is made to the contrary,
the volume listed is the original.

PROPRIETARY RECORDS

Proprietary Records is an artificial title which is ordinarily used
to identify the earliest records of the colony.   They are general
record books covering all sorts of proceedings of the provincial
government, especially records of the Provincial Court.   None of

---

[43] *Arch. Md.,* XV, 26.

[44] *Testamentary Proceedings* 13, 477.

[45] *Ibid.,* 18, flyleaf.

[46] *Arch. Md.,* XI, 113.

the volumes except *Liber Z* is ever found in the early lists of probate records, nor do any of the others contain much probate material. However, they are the only source now existing of such material for the period, 1643-1657, and therefore, have been included in the list below. Even as early as 1673[47] when a list of records relating to testamentary business was made, there were no volume records for the period in question. The list did include seventeen bundles of original papers. Perhaps it had not been considered necessary to record the papers.

Proprietary Record Liber Z, probably the same as the volume called, "G Book of Administrations 1636-1640" in the 1673 list cited above. In later lists it is called "No. 1" and dated from 1637 to 1640. The period actually covered by the volume is December 30, 1637-October 21, 1642 plus several entries dated as late as July 20, 1644, but the erratic chronology of the book and the fact that the last entry is dated 1640 might easily have misled the clerks making the lists. The volume is divided into two parts with several sub-sections in the second part. The pages having been renumbered, both the new and the old page numbers will be indicated in the chart below:

Part 1

    p. 1-85, old p. 1-85, contains all types of records, including scattered entries of testamentary material, Dec. 30, 1637-Sept. 21, 1638.

Part 2

    p. 86, plus 2 pages not numbered, no old page numbers, contains an index to the section following (p. 87-111).

    p. 87-91, old p. 1-5, contains proceedings in probate matters, Oct. 23, 1638-Jan. 12, 1641[2] plus one entry inserted later dated Jan. 16, 1643[4].

    p. 92, blank.

    p. 93-111, old p. 27-45, contains "Administrations & matters perteining thereunto," Nov. 3, 1638-Oct. 21, 1642 plus three entries up to July 20, 1644.

    p. 112, blank.

    p. 113, old p. 59, blank.

    p. 114, contains an index to the inventories below.

[47] See note 43.

p. 115-147, old p. 61-90 (p. 127 is blank, pages facing old p.
87, 88, 89 were not numbered originally), contains "Inventories," 1638-1642.[48]

p. 148, blank.

p. 149, old p. 119, blank.

p. 150, contains an index to the accounts below.

p. 151-164, old p. 121-134, contains "Accompts", 1638-1642.[49]

Proprietary Record Liber P. R., originally known as Liber E, p.
5-200 (p. 1-4 missing), contains mostly records of the Provincial
Court, but also has some Council and Assembly proceedings;
the only testamentary proceedings are several entries regarding
the issuing of letters of administration, Aug. 2, 1642-Feb. 12,
1644[5].

Proprietary Record Liber A, p. 59-359[50] (except that the leaves
containing p. 123-124, 149-150, 277-278, 283-284 are missing; p.
57-58 were present in 1725 when entries from them were transcribed into *Patent Record* Liber No. 2; the leaf containing
p. 396, which completes the volume, and p. 397, which is part
of the index, has been bound into Liber Z above), contents
similar to volume above, but there are more entries relating to
probate matters, May 2, 1647-Mar. 8, 1650[1].

Proprietary Record Liber B, original missing, but practically all
of it was copied by the Commissioners of 1716 as follows:

Liber B, p. 4-23 copied in *Patent Record* Liber No. 1, p. 162-195.

Liber B, p. 29-243 copied in *Patent Record* Liber No. 1, p.
225-640.

Liber B, p. 243-387, plus 2 pages numbered 188-189 and about
50 pages not numbered, copied in *Patent Record* Liber No.
2, p. 133-448.

---

[48] The entries are not in chronological order, but all of them fall within
the dates given.

[49] See note 48.

[50] In the Preface and in the Notes of Volume IV of the *Archives of Maryland,* the editors indicate a belief that the pages missing in front were
removed by Ingle. However, in a list of the pages missing from the
records which were moved from St. Mary's City to Anne Arundel Town
(Annapolis) in 1694, no mention is made of pages missing in the beginning of the volume although pages 123-124, 277-278 and 283-284 are
listed as missing (*Arch. Md.,* XIX, 131). It is inconceivable that the
absence of some fifty odd pages in the beginning of the book would have
been ignored when the lack of single leaves in the middle of the volume
was detected.

The contents of this volume are similar to the one above, but there almost no testamentary entries at all, possibly because such entries were deliberately omitted when the volume was transcribed. The dates are roughly January 1651 to March 1658.

Provincial Court Record Liber S, p. 1-1144, 1157-1158 (pages are incorrectly numbered, but there appear to be no breaks in the text except at the end). Mar. 25, 1658-Jan. 28, 1662[3]. This volume is not generally considered one of the Proprietary Records, but since it contains similar material and is obviously a continuation of Liber B, it has been included here. Probate entries are found only in the first part of the book, dating from March to August, 1658 with two or three entries dated later. In August 1658, a separate series was established for recording such entries. (*See Testamentary Proceedings* 1B).

TESTAMENTARY PROCEEDINGS

Beginning in 1658, the proceedings of the Secretary in probate matters and the proceedings of the Prerogative Court were entered in the series called *Testamentary Proceedings.* As it is now constituted, the series dates from 1657 to 1777. It will be seen in the list below that *Testamentary Proceedings* 1A, 1657, contains a variety of material and is similar to the Proprietary Records. But the rest of the volumes are devoted exclusively to testamentary matters. The earlier volumes were general record books and included wills, inventories and accounts, as well as the proceedings of the Court. In 1674, a separate volume was used for recording inventories and accounts and in 1676, the wills were likewise separated. The series is composed of volumes 1 to 47 running in chronological order.

Testamentary Proceedings 1, composed of the following small volumes which were bound together by the Commissioners of 1716:

1A, Liber P. C. or No. 2, p. 1-12, contains records similar to those in the Proprietary Records above, including land records, cattle marks, 2 wills, 1 inventory and miscellaneous testamentary entries, dates are erratic, but apparently all the entries were made in 1657.

1B, is made up of two small volumes which as early as 1687 had been combined into a single volume called "No. 3". The original volumes were as follows:

p. 1-33, Liber N, contains "Probatts of wills and Letters of Administration with other Businesses concearning Testamentary Causes", Nov. 15, 1659-Apr. 27, 1659[60].

p. 34-55, Liber D, p. 1-22, contents similar to above volume, Aug. 18, 1658-Mar. 23, 1658[9]. This volume, which, of course, should precede the volume above, is the first book to be devoted exclusively to testamentary business.

IC, Liber M or No. 4, p. 1-86, contains all types of testamentary material, Dec. 12, 1660-June 11, 1662.

ID, Liber T or No. 5, p. 1-182, contents similar to above, Mar. 25, 1662-Apr. 2, 1664.

IE, Liber W or No. 6, p. 1-159, contents similar to above, Aug. 20, 1663-Sept. 30, 1665.

IF, Liber GG or No. 7, p. 1-125, contents similar to above, Oct. 20, 1665-July 27, 1666.

Testamentary Proceedings 2, Liber H or No. 8, p. 1-475, contents similar to above, July 8, 1666-June 19, 1668.

Testamentary Proceedings 3, Liber HH or No. 9, p. 1-344, contents similar to above, June 20, 1668-Mar. 26, 1670.

Testamentary Proceedings 4, composed of the following volumes bound together by the Commissioners of 1716:

4A, Liber SS or No. 10, p. 1-57, contains proceedings of a judicial nature only, largely citations and trials of libels, Oct. 2, 1669-Oct. 29, 1674.

4B, Liber No. 11, contents similar to above volume, Aug. 10, 1674-May 3, 1677.

4C, Liber No. 12, contents similar to above volume, May 16, 1677-May 3, 1678.

Testamentary Proceedings 5, Liber No. a, p. 1-545, contains wills, inventories, accounts and other proceedings of a non-judicial nature, Nov. 9, 1670-Sept. 2, 1673.

Testamentary Proceedings 6, Liber P. C. No. C, p. 1-518, contents similar to above volume, Sept. 2, 1673-June 18, 1675.

Testamentary Proceedings 7, Liber No. 13, p. 1-364, contents similar to above volume, except that inventories and accounts were now being recorded in a separate volume, June 18, 1675-Mar. 21, 1675[6].[51]

---

[51] The libers in this period usually stop at the end of the old calendar year See note 7.

Testamentary Proceedings 8, Liber No. 14, p. 1-532, contents similar to above volume, except that wills also were now being recorded in a separate volume, Mar. 31, 1676-Mar. 24, 1676[7]. 8B, p. 1-13, a small section in the back of this volume containing inventories and accounts for 1704.

Testamentary Proceedings 9, Liber No. 15, p. 1-524, contents similar to number 8 above, Mar. 26, 1677-Mar. 22, 1677[8]. 9B, p. 1-22, contents similar to No. 8B above, 1702-1704.

Testamentary Proceedings 10, Liber No. 16, p. 1-378, contains all types of testamentary proceedings, except wills, inventories and accounts, Mar. 27, 1678-Mar. 14, 1678[9]. Since the ensuing volumes in this series are of similar nature, no description will be given of their contents.

Testamentary Proceedings 11, Liber No. 17, p. 1-340, Mar. 26, 1679-Mar. 24, 1679[80].

Testamentary Proceedings 12, two volumes bound together by Commissioners of 1716:
12A, Liber No. 18, p. 1-262, Mar. 30, 1680-Mar. 24, 1680[1].[52]
12B, Liber No. 20, p. 1-311, Mar. 25, 1682-Jan. 25, 1682[3].

Testamentary Proceedings 13, Liber No. 21, p. 1-519, Jan. 26, 1682[3]-Sept. 13, 1687.

Testamentary Proceedings 14, Liber No. 22, p. 1-157, Sept. 13, 1687-July 13, 1689.[53]
14A, Liber LC, p. 1-15, Jan. 14, 1692-Jan. 7, 1692[3].

Testamentary Proceedings 15, three volumes bound together by Commissioners of 1716:
15A, Liber No. 23, p. 1-77, Jan. 7, 1692[3]-Sept. 27, 1693.
15B, no Liber, p. 1-8, Sept. 14, 1692-Dec. 24, 1692.[54]
15C, Liber KC No. 23, p. 1-202, Oct. 2, 1693-May 1, 1695.

Testamentary Proceedings 16, Liber KC No. 24, p. 1-243:
p. 1-50, contain probate proceedings for Calvert County for

[52] Liber No. 19 which must have contained the proceedings for 1681 was missing even then.
[53] During the Revolution of 1689, there was no central probate office and the clerks of the county courts were empowered to perform the necessary duties. For this reason, there is a gap in the proceedings of the Prerogative Court from 1689 to 1692. After the Prerogative Court was re-established, the county clerks were ordered to make a transcript of all the probate proceedings entered in their records during the period in question and send it to the Prerogative Office.
[54] Note that this liber should precede No. 15A.

the period 1689[90]-1692 as returned by the Clerk of Court.[55]
p. 51-54, numbers not used.

p. 55-243, contain proceedings for May 15, 1695-May 27, 1697.

Testamentary Proceedings 17, Liber KC No. 25, p. 1-349, May 29, 1697-Aug. 1, 1699.

Testamentary Proceedings 18, Liber No. 26, two volumes bound together by Commissioners of 1716:

    18A, p. 1-73, Aug. 12, 1699-July 1, 1700.

    18B, p. 1-104, Oct. 8, 1700-Sept. 29, 1701.

Testamentary Proceedings 19, Liber No. W No. 10, three volumes bound together by Commissioners of 1716:

    19A, p. 1-211, Sept. 28, 1701-Oct. 16, 1703.

    19B, p. 1-120, Feb. 20, 1704/5-Mar. 25, 1706.

    19C, p. 1-276, April 1706-Mar. 24, 1708.

Testamentary Proceedings 20, Liber BD, p. 1-89, Oct. 1703-Oct. 1704.[56]

Testamentary Proceedings 21, Liber IC No. 5, p. 1-347, Apr. 1, 1708-April 1711.

Testamentary Proceedings 22, Liber WB No. 8, p. 1-500, April 1711-Oct. 12, 1715. Also a photostat copy.

Testamentary Proceedings 23, Liber WB No. 9, p. 1-402, Oct. 31, 1715-June 22, 1719.

Testamentary Proceedings 24, Liber TB No. 1, p. 3-452, June 26, 1719-July 12, 1721.

Testamentary Proceedings 25, Liber TB No. 9, p. 1-135, July 14, 1721-June 9, 1722.

Testamentary Proceedings 26, Liber AD No. 4, p. 1-235, June 12, 1722-Jan. 21, 1723[4].

Testamentary Proceedings 27, Liber GP No. 5, p. 1-402, Jan. 14, 1723/4-April 22, 1727.

Testamentary Proceedings 28, Liber GP No. 6, p. 1-491, Apr. 27, 1727-July 14, 1730.

Testamentary Proceedings 29, Liber IG No. 7, p. 1-479, July 14, 1730-Jan. 13, 1734[5].

Testamentary Proceedings 30, Liber IG No. 8, p. 1-486, Jan. 14, 1734[5]-Mar. 10, 1738[9].

Testamentary Proceedings 31, Liber WR No. 1, p. 1-679, Mar. 13. 1738[9]-Sept. 8, 1746.

---

[55] See note 53.

[56] Note that this volume should follow No. 19A.

Testamentary Proceedings 32, Liber WR No. 2, p. 1-278, Sept. 9, 1746-July 28, 1749. Also a photostat copy.

Testamentary Proceedings 33, two volumes bound together:
33 Part 1, Liber RD No. 1, p. 1-217, July 31, 1749-Sept. 10, 1750.
33 Part 2, Liber MM No. 1, p. 1-206, Sept. 20, 1752-Dec. 4, 1753.[57]
There is also a photostat copy.

Testamentary Proceedings 34, Liber RD No. 2, p. 1-443, Sept. 11, 1750-July 1751.

Testamentary Proceedings 35, Liber RD No. 3, p. 1-290, July 1751-Sept. 20, 1752.

Testamentary Proceedings 36, Liber MM No. 2, p. 1-446, Dec. 14, 1753-Dec. 27, 1757.

Testamentary Proceedings 37, Liber MM No. 3, p. 1-399, Jan. 10, 1758-Nov. 3, 1760.

Testamentary Proceedings 38, Liber ID No. 1, p. 1-468, Nov. 6, 1760-July 22, 1762.

Testamentary Proceedings 39, Liber ID No. 2, p. 1-535, July 23, 1762-Nov. 7, 1763.

Testamentary Proceedings 40, Liber GM No. 1, p. 1-344, Nov. 8, 1763-Sept. 1764.

Testamentary Proceedings 41, Liber EV No. 1, p. 1-436, Dec. 7, 1764-Oct. 28, 1766.

Testamentary Proceedings 42, Liber EV No. 2, p. 1-405, Oct. 29, 1766-May 5, 1768.

Testamentary Proceedings 43, Liber EV No. 3, p. 1-654, May 6, 1768-Dec. 25, 1770.

Testamentary Proceedings 44, Liber EV No. 4, p. 1-670, Jan. 1, 1771-Dec. 1772.

Testamentary Proceedings 45, Liber EV No. 5, p. 1-370, Jan. 1, 1773-July 9, 1774.

Testamentary Proceedings 46, Liber EV No. 6, p. 1-371, July 1, 1774-Dec. 23, 1775.

Testamentary Proceedings 47, Liber EV No. 7, p. 1-174, Dec. 23, 1775-June 10, 1777.

[57] Note that Part 2 should follow No. 35.

WILLS

The practice of recording wills in separate volumes was begun in 1676. However, the present *Wills* series dates from 1635 to 1777, because the first two volumes are compilations of wills transcribed from various sources. The old liber letters are marked on the spines of the volumes, but the volumes are now designated as Libers 1 to 41 plus one volume called Liber 2A. Libers 12 to 41 run in chronological order, but the chronology of the earlier libers is extremely erratic. Several of the libers have been divided into two volumes, while libers 8, 9 and 10 have been combined into single volume. In all there are 46 volumes in the series.

Wills 1, a compilation of wills extracted from various originals. It was made in 1725 by the Commissioners of 1716. Marginal notes indicate the sources from which the wills were copied. A 1908 handwritten copy and a photostat copy also exist. The chart below will indicate the page number, old reference, new reference and the dates of the wills:

p. 1-9	Liber Z	Prop. Record Liber Z	1637-1643
p. 9-27	Liber A	Prop. Record Liber A	1647-1651
p. 28-67	Liber B	Prop. Record Liber B	1651-1657
p. 67-69	Liber PC No. 2	Test. Proc. 1A	1657
p. 69-114	Liber No. 3	Test. Proc. 1B	1658-1659
p. 114-154	Liber M No. 4	Test. Proc. 1C	1660-1662
p. 154-201	Liber No. 5	Test. Proc. 1D	1662-1663
p. 202-232	Liber No. 6	Test. Proc. 1E	1664-1665
p. 233-260	Liber No. 7	Test. Proc. 1F	1665-1666
p. 260-321	Liber H No. 8	Test. Proc. 2	1666-1668
p. 321-376	Liber HH No. 9	Test. Proc. 3	1668-1669
p. 376-417	Liber No. a	Wills 8	1670-1671
p. 417-553	Liber No. b	Test. Proc. 5	1670-1673
p. 553-639	Liber PC No. c	Test. Proc. 6	1673-1674

Wills 2, also a compilation of wills made in 1726 by the Commissioners of 1716. A photostat copy also exists.

p. 1-81	Liber PC No. C	Test. Proc. 6	1674-1675
p. 82-127	Liber No. 20 or No. D	Wills 2A	1680
p. 127-178	Liber No. E	Wills 2A	1681
p. 179-202	Liber No. F	Wills 2A	1682

p. 202-234	Liber HB No. 6	Inv. & Accts. 11	1690-1692
p. 235-337	Liber KC No. 1	Wills 2A	1693-1694
p. 337-345	Proceedings Book W Annis 1705, 6, 7	Test. Proc. 19C	1707
p. 346-410	Liber PC No. 13	Test. Proc. 7	1675
p. 410	Liber WT anno 1672	Patents No. 17	1671
p. 410-411	Liber MM 1673	Patents No. 18	1669

Wills 2A, four volumes bound together by the Commissioners of 1716. All of it is transcribed in Wills 2.

part 1	Liber D	p. 1-90	1680
part 2	Liber E	p. 1-65	1681
part 3	Liber F	p. 1-50	1682
part 4	Liber KC No. 1	p. 1-146	1693-1694

Wills 3, Liber TB No. 2, in two volumes: part 1— p. 1-368, part 2— p. 369-746, contains inventories and accounts as well as wills, 1703-1706.

Wills 4, Liber No. G, p. 1-319, 1682-1688. A copy transcribed under the provisions of Chapter 147, 1834. The original cannot be found.

Wills 5, Liber A, p. 1-366, 1676-1677, p. 354-366 contain inventories and accounts, 1697-1704.

Wills 6, composed of several volumes of scattered dates:

p. 1-59, Liber H, 1688-1689.

p. 60-61, blank.

p. 62-71, no Liber, 1685-1692, entries not in order.

p. 72-74, blank.

p. 75-408, titled "Wills following K," 1698-1700.

verso p. 1-43, Liber LC, 1692-1693.

Wills 7, Liber K., p. 1-394, 1693-1698. P. 385-394 are handwritten copies, probably made in 1834.

Wills 8, 9 & 10, three volumes bound together by the Commissioners of 1716:

8, Liber No. a, p. 1-209, 1670-1671.

9, Liber No. B, p. 1-114, 1678-1679.

10, Liber No. C, p. 1-87, 1679.

Wills 11, Liber TB, p. 1-484, 1701-1703. Original lacks p. 21-22, 42-45. A transcription made by the Commissioners of 1716 is complete.

Wills 12, two volumes bound together by the Commissioners of 1716:
Liber J. C., p. 1-357, 1705-1709.
Liber W. B. No. 2, p. 1-254, 1709.
There is also a photostat copy.

Wills 13, Liber W. B. No. 5, p. 1-743, 1710-1714. P. 721-740 are handwritten copies, probably made in 1834. P. 741-743 contain the will of Charles, Lord Baltimore, drawn up in 1714. It was recorded in 1907 by order of the Commissioner of the Land Office. There is also a handwritten copy of the whole volume made in 1909.

Wills 14, Liber W. B. No. 6, p. 1-738, 1714-1718.

Wills 15, Liber T. B. No. 1, p. 1-357, 1718-1719. The will of Issabella Drayden, probated in 1719, was recorded on the page facing p. 1 in 1738 by William Rogers, Register.

Wills 16, Liber T. B. No. 5, p. 1-528, 1720-1721. P. 7-10 are copies probably made in 1874. There is also a handwritten copy made in 1909. Ten pages of the original used duplicate page numbers and were copied on p. 736-752 of the copy. However, careful cross references are given in red ink and there is no danger of missing any of these pages.

Wills 17, Liber A. & D. No. 2, p. 1-326, 1721-1722. P. 319-326 contain four wills probated in 1712 which were ordered to be recorded by the Commissary's Court in August 1723.

Wills 18, Liber WB, No. 1, erroneously marked "W.D. No. 1" p. 1-545, 1723-1726. P. 1-40, 546-549 are handwritten copies probably made in 1834.

Wills 19, Liber C.C. No. 2, p. 1-925, 1726-1730.

Wills 20, Liber C.C. No. 3, p. 1-928, 1730-1734.

Wills 21, Liber T&D, p. 1-928, 1734-1738.

Wills 22, Liber D.D. No. 1, p. 1-534, 1738-1742. P. 1-2, 527-534 are handwritten copies, probably made in 1834.

Wills 23, Liber D.D. No. 2, p. 1-700, 1742-1744. P. 7-12 have been transcribed, probably in 1874, and the copies bound in with the originals. A handwritten copy, probably made in 1834, an unbound negative photostat copy and a bound positive photostat copy also are present.

Wills 24, Liber D.D. No. 3, p. 1-551, 1744-1746. P.1-50, 50A, 487-551 are handwritten copies, probably made in 1834. There is also a photostat copy.

Wills 25, Liber D.D. No. 4, p. 1-578, 1746-1748. A transcription probably made in 1834. P. 1-4 appear to be even more recent transcriptions, probably made in 1874. P. 578 ends in the middle of a will, indicating that one or more leaves have been lost at the end of the book.

Wills 26, Liber D.D. No. 5, p. 1-148, 1748-1749. P. 1-2, 19-20, 75-76 are handwritten copies, probably made in 1874. There are two photostat copies, only one of which is bound.

Wills 27, Liber D.D. No. 6, p. 1-541, 1749-1750. P. 1-16, 538-541 are copies probably made in 1834. Also a positive photostat copy.

Wills 28, Liber D.D. No. 7, p. 1-562, 1751-1754. P. 1-16, 465-469, 484-485 are copies, probably made in 1874 or later. There is also a handwritten copy made in 1910.

Wills 29, Liber B.T. No. 1, p. 1-562, 1753-1755. P. 1-32, 559-562 are handwritten copies, probably made in 1834.

Wills 30, Liber B.T. No. 2, two volumes: part 1—p. 1-466, part 2— 467-864, 1755-1760. A transcription, probably made in 1834. P. 265-434 are all that remain of the original.

Wills 31, Liber D.D. No. 1, two volumes: part 1—p. 1-592, part 2— p. 593-1132, 1760-1764. The page numbers now used represent a corrected pagination; the original numbers ran as follows:

   p. 1-592=p. 3-335, 335-512, 613-693.

   p. 593-1097=p. 694-721, 721-787, 787-879, 890-1064, 1067-1160, 1160-1193, 1193-1196, 1196-1205.

   p. 1098—blank.

   p. 1099-1132=p. 1-34, the arrangement of the entries in the old general index to wills indicates that this section was formerly located in the front of the liber, where chronologically it belongs.

Wills 32, Liber S.B. No. 1, p. 1-342, 1764. Also a photostat copy.

Wills 33, Liber C.G. No. 1, p. 1-434, 1764-1765. The pagination has been corrected.

Wills 34, Liber C.G. No. 2, p. 1-479, 1765-1766. P. 1-20 and a page not numbered are handwritten copies, probably made in 1834. There is also a photostat copy.

Wills 35, Liber C.G. No. 3, p. 1-452, 1766-1767.

Wills 36, Liber W.D. No. 1, p. 1-693, 1767-1768.

Wills 37, Liber W.D. No. 2, p. 1-700, 1769-1770.

Wills 38, Liber W.D. No. 3, two volumes: part 1—p. 1-408, part 2— p. 409-902, 1770-1773. The original pagination was faulty and has been corrected.

Wills 39, Liber W.D. No. 4, two volumes: part 1—p. 1-461, part 2— p. 462-901, 1773-1774. The original pagination was faulty and has been corrected, but the present pagination omits number 395 and uses 695 twice.

Wills 40, Liber W.F. No. 1, two volumes; part 1—p. 1-358, part 2— p. 359-743, 1774-1777.

Wills 41, Liber W.F. No. 2, p. 1-509, 1776-1777.

INVENTORIES AND ACCOUNTS

As has already been indicated, a separate series was established for recording inventories and accounts in 1674. The series continued until 1718. In a number of cases, two or three of the original libers have been bound into a single volume. These volumes are now arranged chronologically and numbered from 1 to 39. In addition, volume No. 19½ has been inserted into the series, making a total of 40 volumes.

Inventories & Accounts 1, Liber No. I, p. 1-595, 1674-1675: p. 597-697 contain inventories only 1699-1703.

Inventories & Accounts 2, Liber No. II, p. 1-376, 1676.

Inventories & Accounts 3, Liber No. III, p. 1-172, 1676-1677.

Inventories & Accounts 4, Liber No. IV, p. 1-635, 1677.

Inventories & Accounts 5, Liber No. V, p. 1-475, 1678.

Inventories & Accounts 6, Liber No. VI, p. 1-686, 1679.

Inventories & Accounts 7, three volumes bound together by Commissioners of 1716:

    7A, Liber VII, p. 1-384, 1680.

    7B, Liber VIII, p. 1-214, 1681.

    7C, Liber IX, p. 1-353, 1682.

Inventories & Accounts 8, Liber X, p. 1-523, 1683-1686.

Inventories & Accounts 9, Liber XI, p. 1-518, 1686-1688.

Inventories & Accounts 10, Liber XII, p. 1-495, 1688-1695. Liber LC in back of the volume, p. 1-35, 1692-1693.

Inventories & Accounts 11, Liber HB No. C, two volumes bound together by the Commissioners of 1716:

    11A, p. 1-50 (double pages), contains wills, inventories and administration bonds for Anne Arundel County, 1690-1692.[58]

    11B, p. 1-73, 1700.

Inventories & Accounts 12, Liber KC No. 13, p. 1-160, 1693-1694.

Inventories & Accounts 13, two volumes bound together by the Commissioners of 1716:

    13A, Liber KC No. 14, p. 1-391, 1694-1695.

    13B, Liber KC No. 15, p. 1-157, 1695-1696.

Inventories & Accounts 14, Liber KC No. 16, p. 1-159, 1696-1697.

Inventories & Accounts 15, Liber KC No. 17, p. 1-361, 1697-1698.

Inventories & Accounts 16, Liber KC No. 18, p. 1-247, 1698.

Inventories & Accounts 17, Liber No. 19, p. 1-178, 1698.

Inventories & Accounts 18, Liber No. 20, p. 1-255, 1698-1699.

Inventories & Accounts 19, Liber No. 21, p. 1-179, 1699.

Inventories & Accounts 19½, Liber No. 57, two volumes bound together by the Commissioners of 1716:

    19½A, p. 1-175, 1699-1700.

    19½B, p. 1-160, 1699-1700.

Inventories & Accounts 20, Liber WT, p. 1-274, 1700-1701.

Inventories & Accounts 21, Liber T, p. 1-407, 1701-1702.

Inventories & Accounts 22, Liber WT, p. 1-155, 1702-1703

Inventories & Accounts 23, Liber WT No. 1, p. 1-197, 1702-1703.

Inventories & Accounts 24, Liber WT No. 2, p. 1-292, 1703-1704.

Inventories & Accounts 25, Liber BC No. 3, p. 1-435, 1705-1706.

Inventories & Accounts 26, Liber IC No. 2, p. 1-343, 1706-1707.

Inventories & Accounts 27, Liber IC No. 3, p. 1-264, 1707.

Inventories & Accounts 28, Liber IC No. 44, p. 1-358, 1707-1708.

Inventories & Accounts 29, Liber IC No. 4, p. 1-358, 1707-1708.

---

[58] This liber does not belong in the series, for it is obviously a record of the probate proceedings of the Clerk of the Court for Anne Arundel County during the Protestant Revolution. See note 53.

Inventories & Accounts 30, Liber WB No. 3, p. 1-448, 1709-1710. Also a photostat copy.

Inventories & Accounts 31, Liber WB No. 4, p. 1-446, 1709-1710. Also a photostat copy.

Inventories & Accounts 32, three volumes bound together by the Commissioners of 1716:
>   32A, Liber WB No. 6, p. 1-118, 1710.
>   32B, Liber WB No. 7 & 8, p. 1-272, 1710-1711.
>   32C, Liber WB No. 9, p. 1-174, 1711.

Inventories & Accounts 33, two volumes bound together by the Commissioners of 1716:
>   33A, Liber WB No. 10, p. 1-246, 1711-1712.
>   33B, Liber WB No. 11, p. 1-233, 1712.

Inventories & Accounts 34, Liber WB No. 12, p. 1-246, 1712-1713.

Inventories & Accounts 35, two volumes bound together by the Commissioners of 1716:
>   35A, Liber WB No. 13, p. 1-387, 1713-1714.
>   35B, Liber WB No. 14, p. 1-114, 1713.
>   Also a photostat copy.

Inventories & Accounts 36, three volumes bound together by the Commissioners of 1716:
>   36A, Liber WB No. 15, p. 1-245, 1714.
>   36B, Liber WB No. 16, p. 1-352, 1714-1715.
>   36C, Liber WB No. 17, p. 1-300, 1715-1716.
>   Also a photostat copy.

Inventories & Accounts 37, three volumes bound together by the Commissioners of 1716:
>   37A, Liber WB No. 18, p. 1-203, 1716.
>   37B, Liber WB No. 21, p. 1-243, 1717.
>   37C, Liber WB No. 22, p. 1-161, 1716-1717.

Inventories & Accounts 38, two volumes bound together by the Commissioners of 1716:
>   38A, Liber WB No. 19, p. 1-195, 1716-1717.
>   38B, Liber WB No. 20, p. 1-192, 1717.

Inventories & Accounts 39, three volumes bound together by the Commissioners of 1716:
>   39A, Liber WB No. 25, p. 1-62, 1718.
>   39B, Liber WB No. 24, p. 1-80, 1717-1718.
>   39C, Liber WB No. 23, p. 1-204, 1717.

INVENTORIES

From 1718 until 1777 when the Prerogative Court was abolished, inventories and accounts were recorded in separate volumes. The *Inventories* series is composed of 126 volumes, numbered in chronological order except for 59 and 60 which have been interchanged.

Inventories 1, Liber TB No. 1, p. 1-540, 1718-1719.

Inventories 2, Liber TB No. 3, p. 1-240, 1719.

Inventories 3, Liber TB No. 4, p. 1-351, 1719-1720.

Also a photostat copy.

Inventories 4, Liber TB No. 7, p. 1-356, 1720.

Inventories 5, Liber TB No. 8, p. 1-156, 1720-1721.

Inventories 6, Liber WH No. 1, p. 1-250, 1721.

Inventories 7, Liber AD No. 3, p. 1-357, 1721-1722.

Inventories 8, Liber WB No. 3, p. 1-353, 1722-1723.

Inventories 9, Liber BHAD No. 4, p. 1-455, 1722-1724.

Inventories 10, Liber BHAD No. 5, p. 1-432, 1724-1725.

Inventories 11, Liber BHA No. 6, p. 1-931, 1725-1727.

Inventories 12, Liber CC No. 7, p. 1-541, 1727.

Inventories 13, Liber EHC No. 8, p. 1-481, 1728-1729.

Inventories 14, Liber EHC No. 9, p. 1-358, 1729.

Inventories 15, Liber EHC No. 10, p. 1-736, 1729-1730.

Inventories 16, Liber CC No. 11, p. 1-731, 1730-1732.

Inventories 17, Liber CC No. 12, p. 1-740, 1732-1734.

Inventories 18, Liber T & D No. 1, p. 1-520, 1734.

Inventories 19, Liber T & D No. 2, p. 1-173, 1734.

Inventories 20, Liber DD No. 1, p. 1-541, 1734-1735.

Inventories 21, Liber DD No. 2, p. 1-547, 1735-1736.

Inventories 22, Liber DD No. 3, p. 1-556, 1736-1737.

Inventories 23, Liber DD No. 4, p. 1-542, 1737-1739.

Inventories 24, Liber DD No. 5, p. 1-547, 1739-1740.

Inventories 25, Liber DD No. 6, p. 1-538, 1740-1741.

Inventories 26, Liber DD No. 7, p. 1-588, 1741-1742.

Inventories 27, Liber DD No. 8, p. 1-458, 1742-1743.

Inventories 28, Liber DD No. 9, p. 1-540, 1743-1744.

Inventories 29, Liber DD No. 10, p. 1-453, 1744.

Inventories 30, Liber DD No. 11, p. 1-448, 1744-1745.

Inventories 31, Liber DD No. 12, p. 1-453, 1745.

Inventories 32, Liber DD No. 13, p. 1-353, 1745-1746.

Inventories 33, Liber DD No. 14, p. 1-355, 1746.

Inventories 34, Liber DD No. 15, p. 1-350, 1746-1747.
Inventories 35, Liber DD No. 16, p. 1-545, 1747-1748.
Also a photostat copy.
Inventories 36, Liber DD No. 17, p. 1-268, 1748.
Also a photostat copy.
Inventories 37, Liber DD No. 18, p. 1-445, 1748-1749.
Inventories 38, Liber DD No. 19, p. 1-243, 1749.
Inventories 39, Liber DD No. 20, p. 1-201, 1749.
Also a photostat copy.
Inventories 40, Liber DD No. 21, p. 1-444, 1749.
Inventories 41, Liber DD No. 22, p. 1-533, 1749-1750.
Inventories 42, Liber DD No. 23, p. 1-256, 1750.
Inventories 43, Liber DD No. 24, p. 1-539, 1750.
Inventories 44, Liber DD No. 25, p. 1-445, 1750-1751.
Also a photostat copy.
Inventories 45, Liber DD No. 26, p. 1-252, 1751.
Inventories 46, Liber DD No. 27, p. 1-169, 1751.
Inventories 47, Liber DD No. 28, p. 1-335, 1751.
Inventories 48, Liber DD No. 29, p. 1-550, 1751-1752.
Inventories 49, Liber DD No. 30, p. 1-110, 1752.
Inventories 50, Liber DD No. 31, p. 1-183, 1752.
Inventories 51, Liber DD No. 32, p. 1-166, 1752.
Inventories 52, Liber DD No. 33, p. 1-181, 1752-1753.
Inventories 53, Liber DD No. 34, p. 1-188, 1753.
Inventories 54, Liber DD No. 35, p. 1-346, 1753.
Inventories 55, Liber DD No. 36, p. 1-247, 1753.
Inventories 56, Liber DD No. 37, p. 1-100, 1753.
Inventories 57, Liber BT No. 1, p. 1-451, 1753-1754.
Inventories 58, Liber BT No. 2, p. 1-353, 1754.
Inventories 59, Liber BT & DD No. 2, p. 1-256, 1755.
Inventories 60, Liber BT & DD No. 1, p. 1-744, 1754-1756
Inventories 61, Liber BT No. 1, p. 1-465, 1755-1756.
Inventories 62, Liber BT No. 2, p. 1-272, 1756-1757.
Inventories 63, Liber BT No. 3, p. 1-646, 1757.
Inventories 64, Liber BT No. 4, p. 1-549, 1757-1758.
Inventories 65, Liber BT No. 5, p. 1-531, 1757-1758.
Also a photostat copy.
Inventories 66, Liber DD No. 1, p. 1-365, 1758-1759.
Inventories 67, Liber DD No. 2, p. 1-544, 1759.

Inventories **68,** Liber DD No. 3, p. 1-268, 1759-1760.
Inventories **69,** Liber DD No. 4, p. 1-365, 1759-1760.
Inventories **70,** Liber DD No. A, p. 1-375, 1760.
Inventories **71,** Liber DD No. B, p. 1-181, 1760-1761.
Inventories **72,** Liber DD No. C, p. 1-171, 1761.
Inventories **73,** Liber DD No. D, p. 1-260, 1761.
Inventories **74,** Liber JR No. 1, p. 1-341, 1761.
Inventories **75,** Liber JR No. 2, p. 1-359, 1761.
Inventories **76,** Liber JR No. 3, p. 1-367, 1761.
Inventories **77,** Liber SB No. 1, p. 1-357, 1762.
Inventories **78,** Liber SB No. 2, p. 1-472, 1762.
Inventories **79,** Liber SB No. 3, p. 1-470, 1762.
Inventories **80,** Liber SB No. 4, p. 1-568, 1763.
Inventories **81,** Liber SB No. 5, p. 1-363, 1763.
Inventories **82,** Liber SB No. 6, p. 1-369, 1763-1764.
Inventories **83,** Liber SB No. 7, p. 1-365, 1764.
Inventories **84,** Liber SB No. 8, p. 1-366, 1764.
Inventories **85,** Liber SB No. 9, p. 1-158, 1764.
Inventories **86,** Liber CG No. 1, p. 1-349, 1764-1765.
Inventories **87,** Liber CG No. 2, p. 1-356, 1765.
Inventories **88,** Liber CG No. 3, p. 1-353, 1765.
Inventories **89,** Liber CG No. 4, p. 1-352, 1766.
Inventories **90,** Liber CG No. 5, p. 1-368, 1766.
Inventories **91,** Liber CG No. 6, p. 1-347, 1766-1767.
Inventories **92,** Liber CG No. 7, p. 1-350, 1767.
Inventories **93,** Liber WD No. 1, p. 1-330, 1767.
Inventories **94,** Liber WD No. 2, p. 1-350, 1767.
Inventories **95,** Liber WD No. 3, p. 1-343, 1767-1768.
Inventories **96,** Liber WD No. 4, p. 1-348, 1768.
Inventories **97,** Liber WD No. 5, p. 1-354, 1768.
Inventories **98,** Liber WD No. 6, p. 1-357, 1768-1769.
Inventories **99,** Liber WD No. 7, p. 1-359, 1768-1769.
Inventories **100,** Liber WD No. 8, p. 1-346, 1769.
Inventories **101,** Liber WD No. 9, p. 1-354, 1769.
Inventories **102,** Liber WD No. 10, p. 1-357, 1769.
Inventories **103,** Liber WD No. 11, p. 1-542, 1769-1770.
Inventories **104,** Liber WD No. 12, p. 1-370, 1770.
Inventories **105,** Liber WD No. 13, p. 1-340, 1770-1771.
Inventories **106,** Liber WD No. 14, p. 1-420, 1770-1771.
Inventories **107,** Liber WD No. 15, p. 1-437, 1771.

Inventories 108, Liber WD No. 16, p. 1-435, 1771-1772.
Inventories 109, Liber WD No. 17, p. 1-436, 1772.
Inventories 110, Liber WD No. 18, p. 1-437, 1772-1773.
Inventories 111, Liber WD No. 19, p. 1-435, 1772-1773.
Inventories 112, Liber WD No. 20, p. 1-432, 1772-1773.
Inventories 113, Liber WF No. 1,   p. 1-435, 1773.
Inventories 114, Liber WF No. 2,   p. 1-437, 1773-1774.
Inventories 115, Liber WF No. 3,   p. 1-437, 1773-1774.
Inventories 116, Liber WF No. 4,   p. 1-435, 1773-1774.
Inventories 117, Liber WF No. 5,   p. 1-503, 1774.
Inventories 118, Liber WF No. 6,   p. 1-433, 1774.
Inventories 119, Liber WF No. 7,   p. 1-433, 1774-1775.
Inventories 120, Liber WF No. 8,   p. 1-428, 1774-1775.
Inventories 121, Liber WF No. 9,   p. 1-429, 1774-1775.
Inventories 122, Liber WF No. 10, p. 1-435, 1775-1776.
Inventories 123, Liber WF No. 11, p. 1-426, 1775-1776.
Inventories 124, Liber WF No. 12, p. 1-438, 1776.
Inventories 125, Liber WF No. 13, p. 1-426, 1776.
Inventories 126,   p. 1-85,   1777.

ACCOUNTS

As has been indicated above, the *Accounts* series branched off from the *Inventories and Accounts* in 1718. The series runs to 1777. It is composed of 74 volumes numbered in chronological order.

Accounts 1, Liber TB No. 2, p. 1-446, 1718-1719.
Accounts 2, Liber TB No. 4, p. 1-531, 1719-1720.
Accounts 3, Liber TB No. 6, p. 1-533, 1720-1721.
               Also a photostat copy.
Accounts 4, Liber AD No. 1, p. 1-344, 1721-1724.
Accounts 5, Liber WB No. 2, p. 1-431, 1722-1724.
Accounts 6, Liber BH AD No. 3, p. 1-441, 1724-1725.
Accounts 7, Liber BHA No. 4, p. 1-538, 1725-1726.
Accounts 8, Liber BHA No. 5, p. 1-561, 1726-1728.
Accounts 9, Liber EHC No. 6, p. 1-496, 1728-1729.
Accounts 10, Liber EHC No. 7, p. 1-721, 1729-1731.
Accounts 11, Liber CC No. 8, p. 1-733, 1731-1733.
Accounts 12, Liber CC No. 9, p. 1-770, 1733-1735.
Accounts 13, Liber DD No. 1, p. 1-356, 1735.

Accounts 14, Liber DD No. 2, p. 1-268, 1735-1736; p. 268-543 contain accounts for 1737 beginning where No. 16 ends.

Accounts 15, Liber DD No. 3, p. 1-359, 1736-1737.

Accounts 16, Liber DD No. 4, p. 1-355, 1737-1738.

Accounts 17, Liber DD No. 5, p. 1-541, 1738-1740.

Accounts 18, Liber DD No. 6, p. 1-546, 1740-1742.

Accounts 19, Liber DD No. 7, p. 1-544, 1742-1743.
Also a photostat copy.

Accounts 20, Liber DD No. 8, p. 1-546, 1743-1744.

Accounts 21, Liber DD No. 9, p. 1-449, 1744-1745.

Accounts 22, Liber DD No. 10, p. 1-451, 1745-1746.

Accounts 23, Liber DD No. 11, p. 1-349, 1746-1747.

Accounts 24, Liber DD No. 12, p. 1-322, 1747-1748.
Also a photostat copy.

Accounts 25, Liber DD No. 13, p. 1-270, 1748-1749.

Accounts 26, Liber DD No. 14, p. 1-145, 1748-1749.

Accounts 27, Liber DD No. 15, p. 1-345, 1749-1750.
Also a photostat copy.

Accounts 28, Liber DD No. 16, p. 1-352, 1750.

Accounts 29, Liber DD No. 17, p. 1-242, 1750-1751.

Accounts 30, Liber DD No. 18, p. 1-257, 1751.

Accounts 31, Liber DD No. 19, p. 1-256, 1751.

Accounts 32, Liber DD No. 20, p. 1-419, 1751-1752.
Also a photostat copy.

Accounts 33, Liber DD No. 21, p. 1-451, 1752-1753.

Accounts 34, Liber DD No. 22, p. 1-254, 1753.

Accounts 35, Liber DD No. 23, p. 1-333, 1753.

Accounts 36, Liber BT No. 1, p. 1-547, 1753-1754.

Accounts 37, Liber BT&DD No. 1, p. 1-260, 1754-1755.
Also a photostat copy.

Accounts 38, Liber BT&DD No. 2, p. 1-340, 1755-1756.

Accounts 39, Liber BT No. 2, p. 1-272, 1755-1756.

Accounts 40, Liber BT No. 3, p. 1-361, 1756-1757.

Accounts 41, Liber BT No. 4, p. 1-546, 1757-1758.
Also a photostat copy.

Accounts 42, Liber BT No. 5, p. 1-346, 1758.
Also a photostat copy.

Accounts 43, Liber DD No. 1, p. 1-361, 1758-1759.
Also a photostat copy.

Accounts 44, Liber DD No. 2, p. 1-370, 1759-1760.

Also a photostat copy.

Accounts 45, Liber DD No. 2½, p. 1-53, 1760.

Accounts 46, Liber DD No. A, p. 1-469, 1760-1761.

Accounts 47, Liber IR No. 1, p. 1-471, 1761-1762.

Accounts 48, Liber SB No. 1 & 2, p. 1-463, 1762-1763.

Also a photostat copy.

Accounts 49, Liber SB No. 3, p. 1-645, 1762-1763.

Accounts 50, Liber SB No. 4, p. 1-370, 1763-1764.

Accounts 51, Liber SB No. 5, p. 1-402, 1764.

Accounts 52, Liber CG No. 1, p. 1-348, 1764-1765.

Accounts 53, Liber CG No. 2, p. 1-339, 1765.

Accounts 54, Liber CG No. 3, p. 1-353, 1765-1766.

Accounts 55, Liber CG No.. 4, p. 1-363, 1766-1767.

Accounts 56, Liber CG No. 5, p. 1-352, 1766-1767.

Accounts 57, Liber WD No. 1, p. 1-430, 1767.

Accounts 58, Liber WD No. 2, p. 1-437, 1767-1768.

Accounts 59, Liber WD No. 3, p. 1-427, 1767-1768.

Accounts 60, Liber WD No. 4, p. 1-430, 1768-1769.

Accounts 61, Liber WD No. 5, p. 1-430, 1769.

Accounts 62, Liber WD No. 6, p. 1-430, 1769-1770.

Accounts 63, Liber WD No. 7, p. 1-425, 1769-1770.

Accounts 64, Liber WD No. 8, p. 1-341, 1770.

Accounts 65, Liber WD No. 9, p. 1-341, 1770-1771.

Accounts 66, Liber WD No. 10, p. 1-362, 1771-1772.

Accounts 67, Liber WD No. 11, p. 1-460, 1771-1773.

Accounts 68, Liber WD No. 12, p. 1-346, 1773-1774.

Accounts 69, Liber WF No. 1, p. 1-431, 1773-1774.

Accounts 70, Liber WF No. 2, p. 1-421, 1773-1774.

Accounts 71, Liber WF No. 3, p. 1-444, 1774-1775.

Accounts 72, Liber WF No. 4, p. 1-432, 1774-1777.

Accounts 73, Liber WF No. 5, p. 1-435, 1774-1776.

Accounts 74,   1776-1777.

BALANCE BOOKS

In 1751, another series called *Balance Books* was begun. This series is closely related to the *Accounts*. It shows how the balance remaining in the estate after all necessary payments had been made was distributed to the heirs or representatives. The series covers the period, 1751-1776 and contains seven volumes numbered in chronological order.

Balance Book 1, Liber RD No. 1, p. 1-136 (double pages)
1751-1755.

Balance Book 2, Liber MM No. 1, p. 1-135 (double pages)
1755-1759.

Balance Book 3, Liber MM No. 2, p. 1-181 (double pages)
1759-1763.

Balance Book 4, Liber GM No. 1, p. 1-179
1763-1766.

Balance Book 5, Liber EV No. 1, p. 1-403 (p. 1-157 double pages)
1766-1770.

verso p. 1-27 is a Book of Entry for all papers returned to the Prerogative Office by the Deputy Commissaries, 1767.

Balance Book 6, Liber EV No. 2, p. 1-354   1770-1774.
Balance Book 7, Liber EV No. 3, p. 1-78   1775-1776.

ORIGINAL PAPERS

When the Register of Wills for Anne Arundel County distributed the original papers of the Prerogative Court to the various counties in 1779 and 1783, he naturally retained the papers relating to Anne Arundel in his own custody. He also retained various other papers which belonged to the Prerogative Court proper. By the time these papers were transferred to the Land Office, they were regarded as a single collection. The distinction between the two types of papers had been forgotten or was no longer considered important. The papers are now divided on a different basis. One group contains wills only and is called *Original Wills*. They are arranged alphabetically and the wills filed under each letter are numbered from one to the end. All the other papers have been grouped together under the heading *Testamentary Papers*. They include administration bonds, inventories, accounts, libels, summons, commissions, deputy commissaries' returns, etc. The papers are arranged chronologically except that all the papers relating to an estate are filed together.

Testamentary Papers, 96 boxes, 1659-1777.
Original Wills, 32 boxes, 1666-1777.

INDEXES

Except for a general index of wills listed in 1776,[59] there appear to have been no other indexes to the Prerogative Court Records than the self-contained indexes which may still be found in practically all of the volumes. Even that index seems to have disappeared by 1874, for in that year the Register of Wills for Anne Arundel County was authorized to make an index to the will books.[60] This was the only general index until 1894, when $1,500 was appropriated for making indexes to the other series.[61] This amount proved insufficient, particularly since part of it was set aside for rearranging and jacketing the original wills. Therefore, additional sums were appropriated in 1896[62] and 1898[63] for completing the job. As a result of this effort, general indexes were provided for all of the Prerogative Court series, except the *Testamentary Proceedings*. The indexing of this series was also begun and libers 1-26 were completed. No further work was done until the records were turned over to the Land Office.

From 1904 to 1906, the indexing of libers 27-30 was completed by John B. League, apparently of his own initiative, for it was not until 1906 when the work had already been finished that the General Assembly appropriated the money to pay him.[64] After a lapse of twenty years, the Commissioner of the Land Office reported in 1926 that the indexing of liber 31 was nearly completed.[65] By 1932, thirteen more volumes had been done.[66] Ths three libers remaining were indexed before December 1935, for the index was complete when it was transferred to the Hall of Records.

Meanwhile, a card index to wills had been made during the biennium 1932-1934.[67] A new index to accounts was also made, but the typing of the cards had only been partially completed when they were turned over to the Hall of Records.

---

[59] *Arch. Md.*, XI, 114.
[60] *Laws of Md.*, 1874, ch. 381.
[61] *Ibid.*, 1894, ch. 441.
[62] *Ibid.*, 1896, ch. 34.
[63] *Ibid.*, 1896, ch. 237.
[64] *Ibid.*, 1906, ch. 303.
[65] *Triennial Report of the Commissioner of the Land Office of Maryland from October 1, 1923 to September 30, 1926*, p. 12.
[66] *Biennial Report of the Commissioner of the Land Office of Maryland from October 1, 1930 to September 30, 1932*, p. 17.
[67] *Biennial Report of the Commissioner of the Land Office of Maryland from October 1, 1932 to September 30, 1934*, p. 17.

From 1935 to 1946, the Hall of Records completed the work of transferring the remaining volume indexes to cards, making many corrections. In addition, the *Testamentary Papers* were arranged and indexed on cards.

The indexes are based on the name of the decedent except the card index to *Accounts,* which includes the name of the administrator or executor as well, and the index to *Testamentary Proceedings,* which is an all-name index. The card indexes are filed under two headings: *Testamentary Proceedings,* which contains only the cards referring to the *Testamentary Proceedings* series and *Testamentary References,* which includes all the other cards referring to Prerogative Court Records.

Index to Testamentary Proceedings, 1657-1777, 19 volumes and card index.

Index to Wills, 1635-1777, 4 volumes (2 sets of 2 volumes each, one set handwritten and the other typed) and card index.

Index to Inventories and Accounts, 1674-1718, 2 volumes and card index.

Index to Inventories, 1718-1777, 3 volumes and card index.

Index to Accounts, 1718-1777, 2 volumes and card index.

Index to Balance Books, 1751-1776, 1 volume and card index.

Index to Original Wills, 1666-1777, 1 volume and card index.

Index to Testamentary Papers, 1659-1777, card index.

LIST OF COLONIAL PROBATE OFFICERS

A list of the colonial probate judges and their clerks or registers has been included here, because they are frequently mentioned in the records and it is interesting and useful to know who was serving at a given date and how long he served, especially since the initials of the judges or the registers were often used in the original liber lettering of the individual volumes. As has already been indicated, the officers who had jurisdiction over probate matters during the colonial period were the Secretaries of the Province up to 1673 and the Commissaries General afterwards. Their commissions were consistently recorded: the Secretaries in the proceedings of the Governor and Council and the Commissaries in the proceedings of the Prerogative Court. Occasionally, the Governor assumed the duties of probate judge himself. Whenever this happened, the name of the Governor, prefixed by his title has been inserted in the list.

The appointments of the clerks or registers were also faithfully recorded after 1685, but before then the appointments were rarely entered in the records. It was necessary to compile the list of the early clerks from the occasional reference to them found in the records. Therefore it would not be surprising if some errors or omissions have occurred.

JUDGES

Secretaries of the Province

John Lewger	1637-1647
Thomas Hatton	1648-1654
William Durand	1654-1656
Richard Preston	1656
Philip Calvert	1656-1660
Henry Coursey	1660-1661
Henry Sewall	1661-1665
Gov. Charles Calvert	1665-1666
Richard Boughton	1666
Gov. Charles Calvert	1666-1669
William Calvert	1669-1670
William Talbot	1670-1671
Gov. Charles Calvert	1671-1673

Commissaries General

Philip Calvert	1673-1682
William Digges and Col. Henry Darnall	1683-1685
Henry Darnall and Clement Hill	1685-1689
(Revolution of 1689, see note 53.)	
Gov. Lionel Copley	1692
Nehemiah Blackiston	1692-1693
Kenelm Cheseldyn	1693-1699
John Addison, John Courts and Thomas Brooke	1699-1700
Thomas Brooke	1700-1704
Thomas Brooke and William Dent	1704-1705
Thomas Brooke and John Contee	1705-1708

William Bladen	1708-1718
Thomas Bordley	1718-1721
William Holland	1721
William Holland, Thomas Addison and Daniel Dulany	1721-1722
Thomas Brooke, William Holland, Thomas Addison and Daniel Dulany	1722-1724
Thomas Brooke, William Holland and Thomas Addison	1724-1727
William Holland, Philip Lee and Thomas Brooke, Jr.	1727
Charles Calvert	1727-1728
Edward Henry Calvert	1728-1730
Charles Calvert	1730-1734
Benjamin Tasker and Daniel Dulany	1734
Daniel Dulany	1734-1753
Benjamin Tasker	1753-1754
Benjamin Tasker and Daniel Dulany	1754-1758
Daniel Dulany	1759-1761
John Ridout	1761-1762
Stephen Bordley	1762-1764
Charles Goldsborough	1764-1767
Walter Dulany	1767-1773
William Fitzhugh	1773-1777

CLERKS OR REGISTERS

Clerks of the Secretary's Office

William Bretton	1647-1657
Thomas Turner	1657-1658
William Bretton	1658-1660
Peter Bathe	1660-1661
John Gittings	1661-1664
Daniel Jenifer	1664-1668
John Blomfield	1669-1670
Thomas Cakewood	1670-1671
Robert Ridgely	1671-1673

Clerks and Registers of the Prerogative Court

Michael Rockford	1674-1676
William Stone	1676-1678
William Cornwaleys	1678-1679
James Boullay	1679
John Thompson	1679-1681
George Butler	1681-1682
Eustachius Turin	1682-1685
James Cullen	1685
William Taylard	1685-1687
James Heath	1687-1688
John Blomfield	1688-1689
(Revolution of 1689, see note 53.)	
John Llewellin	1692-1694
John Bouye	1694-1698
Edward Batson	1698-1699
William Bladen	1699-1700
William Taylard	1700-1706
Thomas Bordley	1706-1712
Evan Jones	1712-1713
Benjamin Tasker	1713-1718
John Beard	1718
Philip Hammond	1718-1719
Vachel Denton	1719-1723
George Plater	1723-1729
John Gibson	1729-1736
William Rogers	1736-1749
Richard Dorsey	1749-1752
Michael Macnemara	1752-1760
John Davidge	1760-1764
Gideon McCauley	1764
Elie Vallette	1764-1777

INDEX

Jenifer, Daniel, Clerk of Secretary's
Office, 117.
Jones, Evan, Clerk and Register of Pre-
rogative Court, 118.
Judge for probate of wills. See Commis-
sary General.
Judge of Land Office, powers and duties,
19-20; prepares annual list of patents, 37.
See also Register of Land Office.
Kent, Isle of, *Rent Rolls*, 60.
Kent County, *Rent Rolls*, 61, 64, 66; *Debt
Books*, 71-72, 75.
Kilty, William, analysis of rent-roll and
debt-book recording, 37-38.
Land, source of wealth for Proprietor, 13.
Land administration, history of, 15-20;
comparison of Eastern and Western
Shore methods, 41.
Land Council, created, 18; weakened, 19;
proceedings of, 57.
Land Office, established, 18; private
versus public nature, 19; additional records found elsewhere, 21 f. 22; development of record series, 29-30; custody of
original papers of Prerogative Court,
113; indexing of Prerogative Court
records, 114;
Commissioner of: custodian of Prerogative Court records, 91; orders recording of will of Charles, Lord Baltimore, 102;
records: custody of, 42; list prepared
(1680), 77.
League, John B., indexing of *Testamentary Proceedings*, 114.
Leaseholders, status of, 15.
Lee, Philip, Commissary General, 117.
Lewger, John, Sr., entered colony (1637),
23; Secretary, 16, 83, 116; Surveyor, 25.
Lewger, John, Jr., entered colony (1637),
23.
Lewis, William, certificate of survey, 25.
Lindsey, James, special warrant, 24.
Linnis, Phillip, entered colony (1637), 23.
Llewellin, John, Register of Land Office,
18, 77; Clerk and Register of Preroga-
tive Court, 118.
Lloyd, Philemon, first Judge or Register of

Land Office after proprietary restora-
tion, 19.
Lord Baltimore. See Calvert.
Lord Proprietor. See Proprietor.
Lowe, Nicholas, Proprietor's land agent,
36.
McCauley, Gideon, Clerk and Register of
Prerogative Court, 118.
Macnemara, Michael, Deputy Commissary
for Anne Arundel County, 89 f. 30;
Clerk and Register of Prerogative Court,
118.
Manors, defined, 14; how recorded, 17;
plats of Proprietor's, 33.
Manor leases, explained, 28-29.
Manor rents, defined, 13-14; annual yield,
14.
Orchard, Nathaniel, demand of land, 24.
Original Papers of Prerogative Court,
custody of after Revolution, 90.
Original Papers, Prerogative Court, list
and analysis of, 113.
Original Wills, described, 113; *Index to*,
115.
Orphans' estates, jurisdiction of county
courts, 87.
Overseers, status of, 15.
Patents, earliest evidence of, 15; record-
ing of, 16; how obtained, 17; nature of,
23-26.
Patents, contents of, 21; description of,
30; custody of, 42; list and analysis of,
44-56; *Index to*, 76 and f. 88.
Peake, George, patent, 25.
Peale, Saint George, Register of Land
Office, 56.
Pike, Ann, entered colony (1637), 23.
Plater, George, Clerk and Register of Pre-
rogative Court, 118.
Plats of Proprietor's Manors, 33.
Pope, Nathan, appraiser, 88.
Prerogative Court, development of, 82;
first use of title, 84-85; legal back-
ground, 87.
Prerogative Court records, indexes to,
114-115.
Preston, Richard, Secretary, 116.

neglect of record of proprietary leases, 31-32.

Sheriffs, collected rents, 35, 36.

Ships: *Ark*, *Dove*, 22; *Unity*, 23.

Somerset County, *Rent Rolls*, 61-62, 67; *Debt Books*, 73, 74, 75.

Special warrants, explained, 24.

Stone, William, Clerk and Register of Prerogative Court, 118.

Surplus warrants, explained, 27-28.

Surveyor General, office established (1641), 16-17; how appointed, 20; prepares rent rolls, 35.

Talbot, Sir William, Secretary, 84, 116.

Talbot County, *Rent Rolls*, 62, 67; *Debt Books*, 74, 75.

Tasker, Benjamin, Commissary General, 117; Clerk and Register of Prerogative Court, 118.

Taylard, William, Clerk and Register of Prerogative Court, 118.

Testamentary Papers, described, 113; *Index to*, 115.

Testamentary Proceedings, list and analysis of, 95-99; *Index to*, 115.

Thompson, John, Clerk and Register of Prerogative Court, 118.

Tilghman, Col. Edward, receipt of rent rolls and other records, 40-41.

Turin, Eustachius, Clerk and Register of Prerogative Court, 118.

Turner, Thomas, Clerk of Secretary's Office, 117.

Upper Marlboro, Prerogative Court records removed from, 90.

Vallette, Elie, Register of Wills for Anne Arundel County, efforts to obtain custody of Prerogative Court records, 89-90; Clerk and Register of Prerogative Court, 118.

Warrants, preliminary to patent, 17; types of, 24-25; explained, 26-27.

Warrants, contents of, 21; description of, 30; custody of, 42; list and analysis of, 56-59; *Index to*, 76 and f. 88.

Western Shore rent rolls, 40, 41.

Western Shore Treasurer, custodian of Land Office records, 42.

Whitehead, Mary, entered colony (1637), 23.

Willan, Richard, special warrant, 24.

Williamson, Martha, entered colony (1637), 23.

Wills, list and analysis of, 100-104; *Index to*, 115.

Wills, original. See *Original Wills*.

Worcester County, *Rent Rolls*, 67; *Debt Books*, 74, 75.

www.ingramcontent.com/pod-product-compliance
Lightning Source LLC
Chambersburg PA
CBHW031130020426
42333CB00012B/308